The A to Z Book of Weeds and Other Useful Plants

A Beginner's Guide

Michael P. Earney

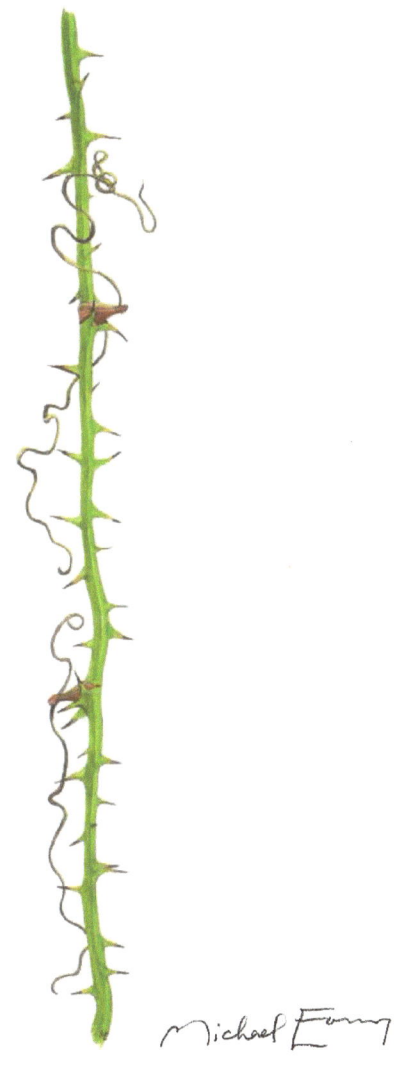

Copyright Michael P. Earney 2019 All Rights reserved.

No part of this book may be reproduced, stored in a retrieval system, or transmitted by any means, electronic, mechanical, photocopying, recording, or otherwise, without written permission from the author.

ISBN-13: 978-1-941345-70-2 HB
ISBN-13: 978-1-941345-71-9 PB
Second Edition

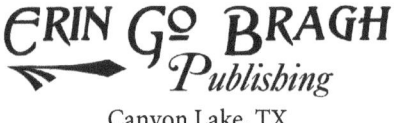

Canyon Lake, TX

Cover painting of Greenbrier (*Smilacaceae*) by Michael Earney.

The tender young tips of the greenbrier make a tasty treat when out in the woods or a handful can be collected in little time then steamed to accompany any meal.

Cover design, book design and layout by Michael Earney and Lynn Amos.

Dedication

Dedicated to June North, who generously allowed me to invade her studio and furnished the materials used to produce most of the paintings in this book, and to Lynn Amos, without whom this book might never have seen the light of day.

"Gather ye rosebuds while ye may; Old time is still a-flying.
And this same flower that smiles today
Tomorrow will be dying."

Robert Herrick (1591 - 1674)

Acknowledgements

My thanks are given to family and friends who fed and housed me during the process of producing this book. For input and encouragement, Carol Elliott, Lynn Amos, Delena Tull, and all those wild plant gatherers that have gone before me.

Several of these paintings were intended for an "edible plants of Texas" calendar which was never produced and are used here in the spirit of recycling.

Weeds

Weeds, those pesky plants we throw away,
we slash, we burn, dig up and spray.
What good are they? You may well ask.
To answer this is no small task.
Herein, you'll find a small selection.
To point you in the right direction.
If you get sick, are taken ill,
you have a sprain or take a spill,
it's to the weeds for help, you first should turn.
There, remedies abound, you'll quickly learn.
Take roots, leaves, stalks, flowers, fruits, and seeds.
The things you need are in the weeds.
Michael P. Earney 2019

Disclaimer

This book is intended to provide general information only. Information provided is not designed to diagnose, prescribe, or treat any illness, or injury. Always consult a health care professional or medical doctor when suffering from any health ailment, disease, illness, or injury, or before attempting any traditional or folk remedies.

Some Texas Folk Remedies

From Brazos County: Teething, "Pick some yard percy (purslane) and crunch it up to obtain the milk. Rub this on the gums."

From Tarrant County: "Use dandelion tea as a cough medicine."

From Brazos County: Rheumatism, "Bind the joint with a hot prickly pear poultice."

From Maverick County: Stomach ache, "Grind green mesquite beans into a pulpy dough and eat the dough."

From Coryell County: Dysentery, "Chew oak leaves."

From Bexar County: Colds, "Put some mesquite leaves under your hat."

If you don't believe in the medicinal properties of plants try this from Van Zandt County: "Rub the wart with a screwdriver and carry the screwdriver in your pocket."

N.B. For recipes, directions, warnings and other useful information, refer to the books listed in the bibliography. These and the many other fine books on wild plants will help you in finding and using wild weeds.

Introduction

Long before the dawn of agriculture, believed by some to be 11,000 years ago, mankind's main source of food and medicine was wild plants. Foods gathered in the wild still form the basis of many people's diet and nearly two-thirds of the world's 7.3 billion people depend on plant-based traditional medicine. The healers that administer such medicines call upon a store of knowledge that has been handed down for centuries combined with first-hand observation and familiarity with the plants. This means that he or she knows when, where and what part of the plant to pick for any particular ailment. It is these variables that make it difficult for modern medicine to duplicate the healing properties of some medicinal plants; let alone the fact that folk medicine often requires cleansing ceremonies, ritual chanting, the laying-on of hands and many other esoteric procedures as part of the diagnosis and treatment.

Nevertheless, certain medicines derived from plants have made their way into the modern pharmacopoeia, quinine being, perhaps, the best known of these. The bark of the Cinchona tree from South America provides this anti-malaria drug. Less known is the fact that White Willow bark, used to treat fevers, was found to contain salicylic acid, the active ingredient in aspirin. The opium poppy, foxglove, valerian and many more are still the source of ingredients used in modern medicine.

Many others are being examined and tested to see if they can provide cures for diseases that known drugs cannot cure. Ethnobotanists continue to search for plants with healing powers; given that there are about 400,000 species of plants, including mosses and algae, in the world, many of which are endangered, disappearing or may already be extinct, the search for those that might hold the power to save lives has become a race against time.

The fact that we ignore or destroy plants that could provide medicine, food, shelter and energy to millions of people should be of concern to everyone. As stated elsewhere in this book, much money and effort is spent eradicating plants that, if properly utilized, could afford better food and materials than their cultivated equivalents. At the same time some wild medicinal plants are being over-harvested. American Wild Ginseng is in such great demand in Asia that poachers participate in black market exports of the plant.

While it is unlikely that gathering plants for personal use will severely impact any particular species, there are those that are endangered and it is important to know them. Even those that appear to be abundant should be gathered with the awareness that over-harvesting could lead to a shortage and even the loss of that species.

There is really nothing more satisfying or enjoyable than to go out and find plants that you can eat or make something useful with. Edible wild plants often grow in great abundance, though rarely gathered they are delicious and free! Eat only plants you have positively identified as edible and you know to be safe. How to do that? Well, this book is designed to help. If they are growing near buildings or along roadsides they may have been sprayed with pesticides, the soil along heavily trafficked roads may be contaminated by vehicle emissions. Plants growing in polluted water could also be contaminated. So wash, boil or disinfect these plants. Some plants have naturally occurring concentrations of compounds that can upset your stomach and some people will be allergic to a plant that is perfectly fine for someone else. Avoid spoiled fruit. This goes just as much for foods found in the house.

Some weeds are easy to identify, just as are some mushrooms, but be sure before you eat anything you find. Get to know the different types of leaves, the size of the bush or tree and the kinds of locations where particular plants can generally be found.

Roots, tubers, bulbs and rhizomes are edible and can help you identify a plant. Remember that some plants have edible *and* poisonous parts, while others are only edible at certain times in their life cycle or after being cooked.

Never eat anything you are not certain about and it's better to eat only a little until you know if it is going to upset you—this can take up to 24 hours. Be careful, be cautious, be sure, then you can enjoy taste treats you won't find in the store.

Take a bag or two with you. It's best to wear a long sleeve shirt, long pants, boots and a hat when you are out in the woods; these will protect you from poison ivy and other irritating plants. (If you do come into contact with poison ivy, get that resin off as soon as possible. Cucumber, apple cider vinegar, aloe vera and even watermelon rind will all relieve the itch. Wash those clothes and your dog if it goes with you, the resins can remain harmful for weeks). Always look where you are going. Looking for wild plants will help you become aware of your surroundings. You will see things you didn't know were there. Happy hunting or, we should say, happy gathering!

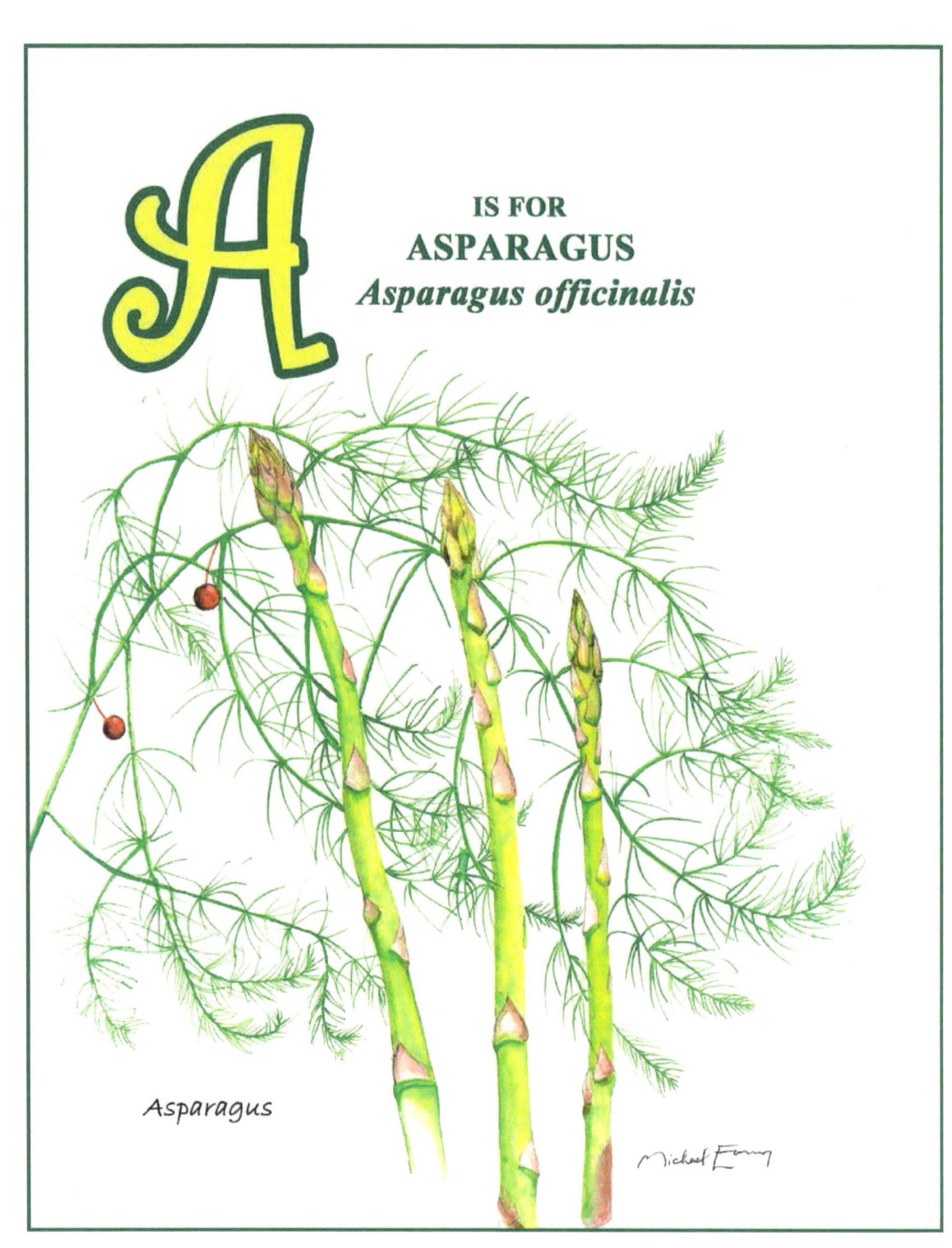

Asparagus is a perennial, so once you find where it grows you can go back year after year; the young, slender asparagus spears appear in the spring. Pick them when they are five to eight inches tall. You'll soon learn whether it's okay to pick them shorter or longer, just take a bite! If you don't have a knife just snap the stalk near the ground; if it's hard to snap slide your hand up until you reach the place where it snaps easily or you can just pull it out of the ground. The soft delicate foliage of the mature plant which grows to about three-feet high has small red berries and later, when it's dried out, will stay through the winter and if you have forgotten where it was, can lead you back to this delicious food. If you are lucky enough to find them in great abundance, by all means give some to friends and eat a lot but you can also can them.

Cool fact: Asparagus provides protein, folates and vitamins A, C and K. It's the sulphurous compounds in asparagus that makes your pee smell funny, or should I say, 'adds the distinctive odor to your urine,' but be glad you smell them because it means your sense of smell is working. Some people don't smell them and never have that wonderful reminder of a tasty meal.

What other wild plants start with A?

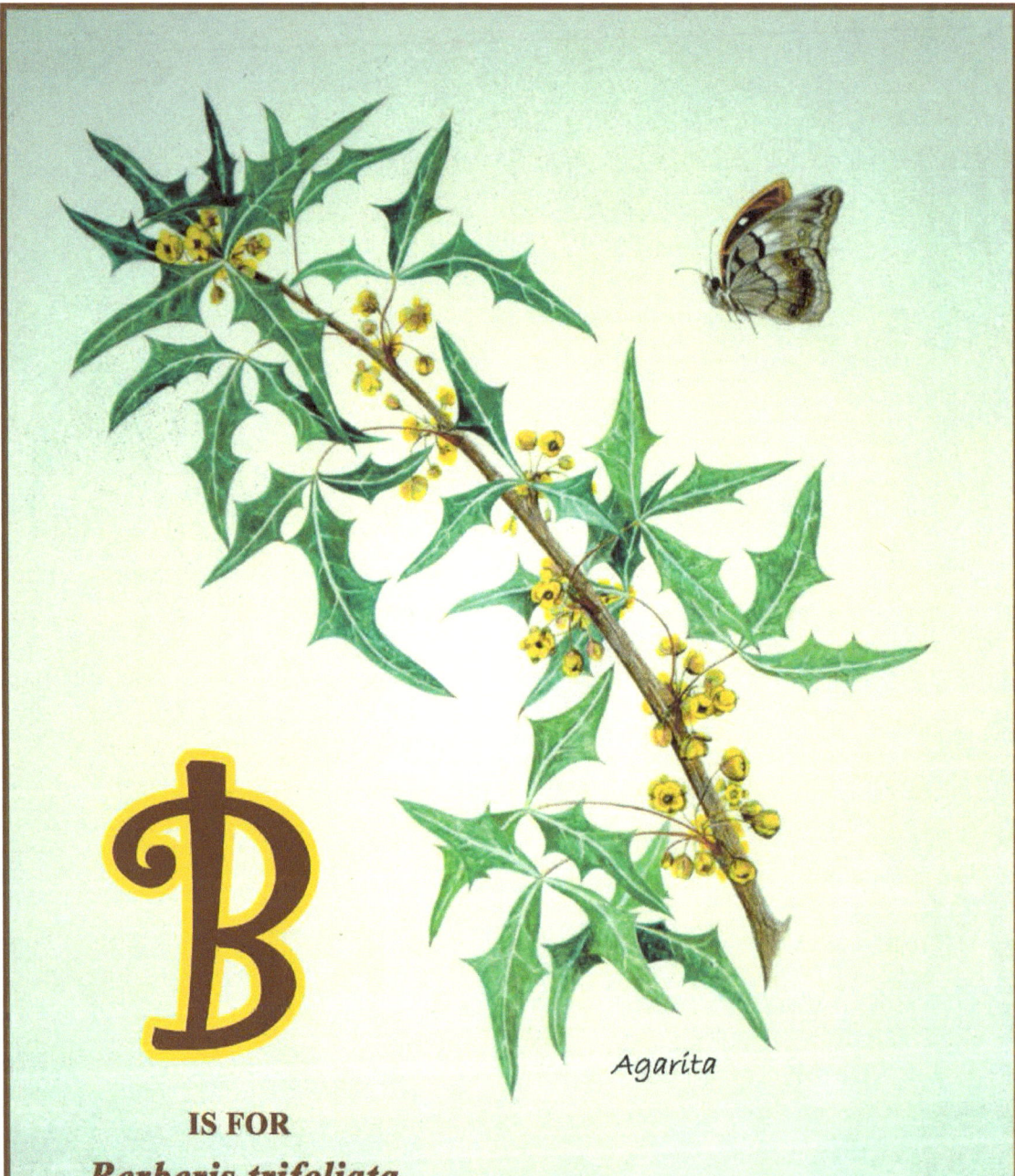

Agarita

B

IS FOR
Berberis trifoliata

Berberis, commonly known as agarita, algerita or algarito, is an evergreen shrub which is fairly common in Texas; there are two others that are rare and should be left alone. You might feel that you would just as soon leave the trifoliata alone too since the stiff spiny leaves make gathering its small red berries difficult. I have imagined Native Americans spreading buckskins under and around the shrub and beating it with a stick to get the ripe berries to fall off, which they do readily. The berries have a tart flavor so you probably won't want to eat too many raw. Getting enough to make a cool refreshing drink or for jellies or pies is definitely a challenge.

The fragrant yellow flowers make an early spring walk delightful with their hint that spring is almost here. Various Indian tribes used, and may still use, the plant medicinally: the root for skin or gum problems; as an eyewash; to treat scorpion bites and as a laxative; the leaves and twigs for stiff joints. The yellow wood makes a yellow dye.

Cool fact: Crushed agarita berries were used for face paint and for painting ceremonial objects by the Zuni Indians. The plant belonged to and was reserved for the exclusive use of those in charge of the ki-wit-siwe (Stevenson).

Ki-wit-siwe, I believe is a phonetic spelling of the Zuni name of the ceremonial chamber better known as a kiva, a Hopi word.

What other plant names start with B?

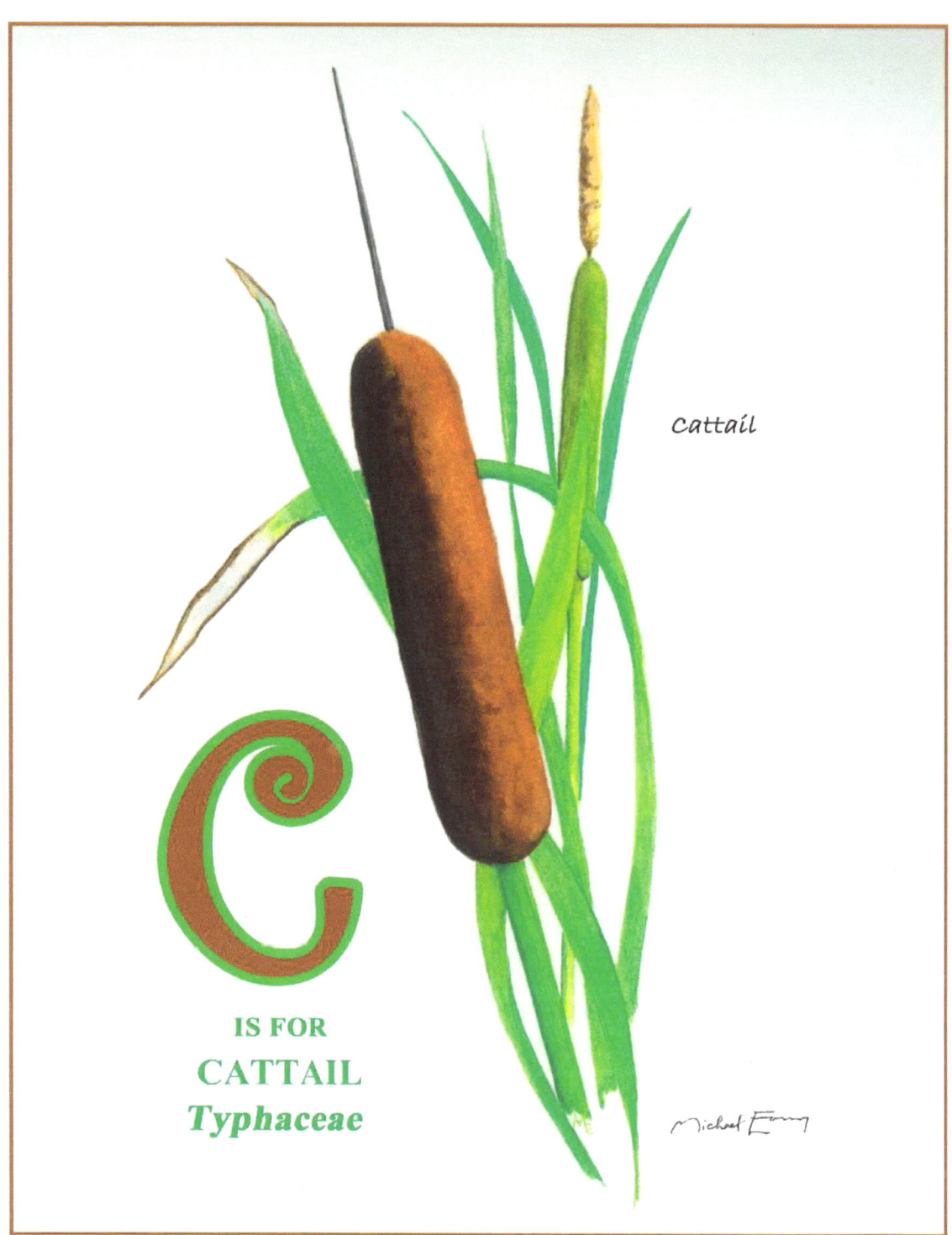

Cattails are not just for decoration. There is a meal to be had from every part of the plant beginning early in the spring when the first new shoots are rising from the old standing leaves. Just as when you pull on the top part of blades of grass, the bottom of the strand is soft and edible. This part, which may be six to eight inches long, is called Russian or Cossack asparagus; it can be eaten raw or boiled. You may have to get wet gathering cattails because they are found either in a pond or on the water's edge. When the familiar flowers appear, they don't look like flowers, but they are; the top spike is the male. The bottom spike, holding the female flowers, can be cut off while still green, boiled, buttered and eaten like corn on the cob. The pollen from the male flower is high in protein. Shake the pollen into a bag and it can be added to flour for cakes and bread. If you are allergic to pollen don't use it. You'd have to be really hungry to want to separate the seeds from the cattail fluff. The same goes for the other end, the roots; you can't eat them raw and processing them for the starch is a lot of work, even though they contain as much protein as rice or corn and more carbohydrate than potatoes. Chair-seating can be woven with the leaves and stems. It is considered very invasive, but rather than poisoning it, ethanol could be produced: an abundant biofuel is waiting to be used.

Cool fact: On Lake Titicaca in Bolivia, the local lake dwellers live on floating islands that they weave of cattails and bulrushes.

What other wild plants start with C?

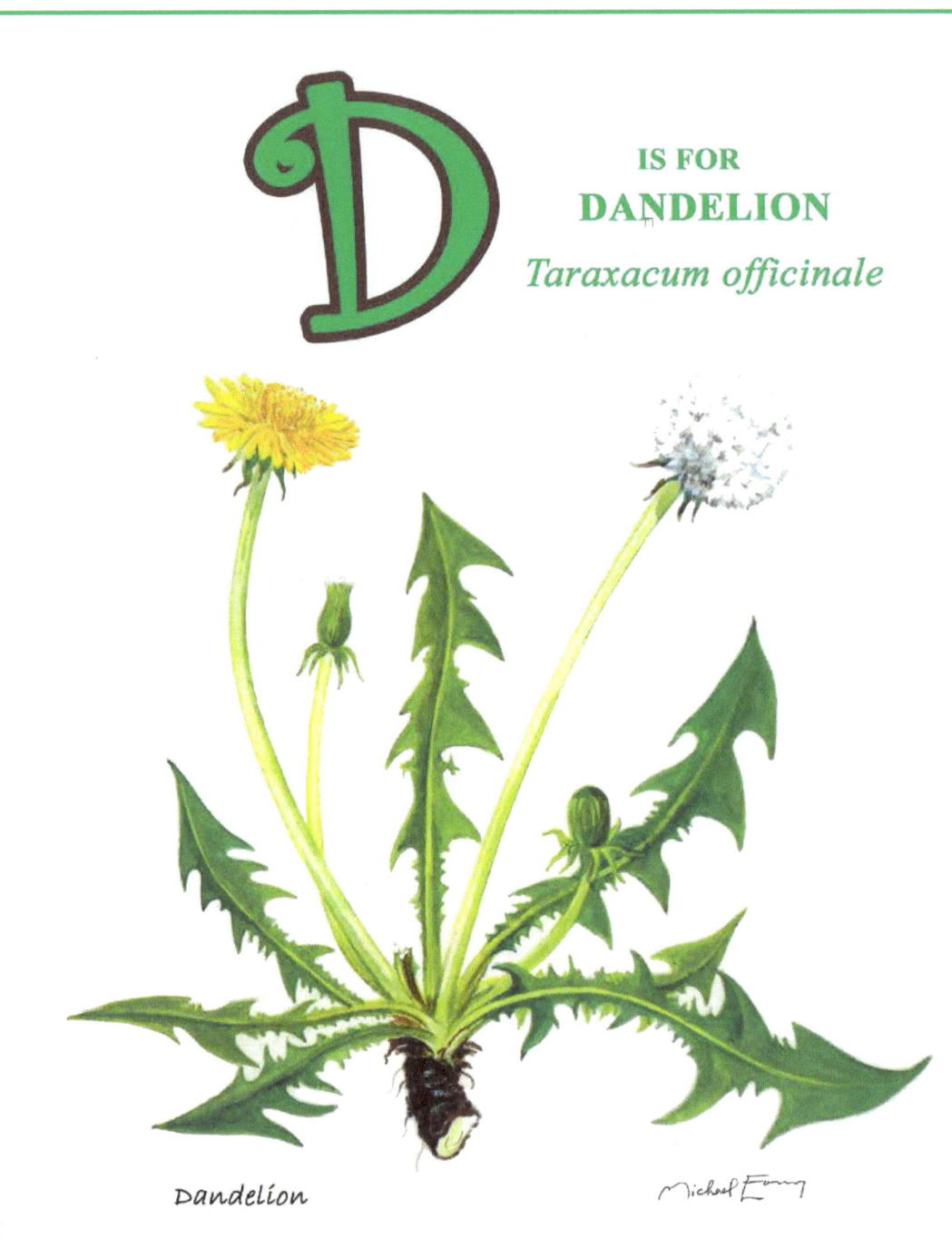

Dandelion is the plant just about everyone agrees is a weed: blowball, pissabed, priest's crown, swine's snout and tell time are some of its folk-names. Much time and money is spent trying to eradicate it. Weed or not, it is well known that the dandelion is edible from the root to the flower and its use medicinally has been recorded for at least a thousand years. The English name, dandelion, comes from the French dent-de-leon which comes from the Latin, dens leonis (lion's tooth) which is attributed to the shape of the leaves, the roots, or its flowers, take your pick.

The young green leaves can be used in salads or cooked; boiling them two or three times will get the bitterness out. The unopened flowers can be added to pancakes; the opened flowers can be fried in tempura batter. The root is the part most used medicinally. It's said to cleanse the blood, increase the volume of bile which helps the liver, kidneys and pancreas. The root can be fried or steamed and eaten like parsnip. Most often it is dried and ground to make a coffee substitute. Dandelion wine is made with the flowers and a beer can be made with the leaves.

Cool fact: The 16th century herbalist Petrus Andreas Matthiolus wrote, "Magicians say that if a person rub[sic] himself all over with dandelion he will everywhere be welcome and obtain what he wishes." I wonder if anyone actually tried that.

What other wild plant starts with D?

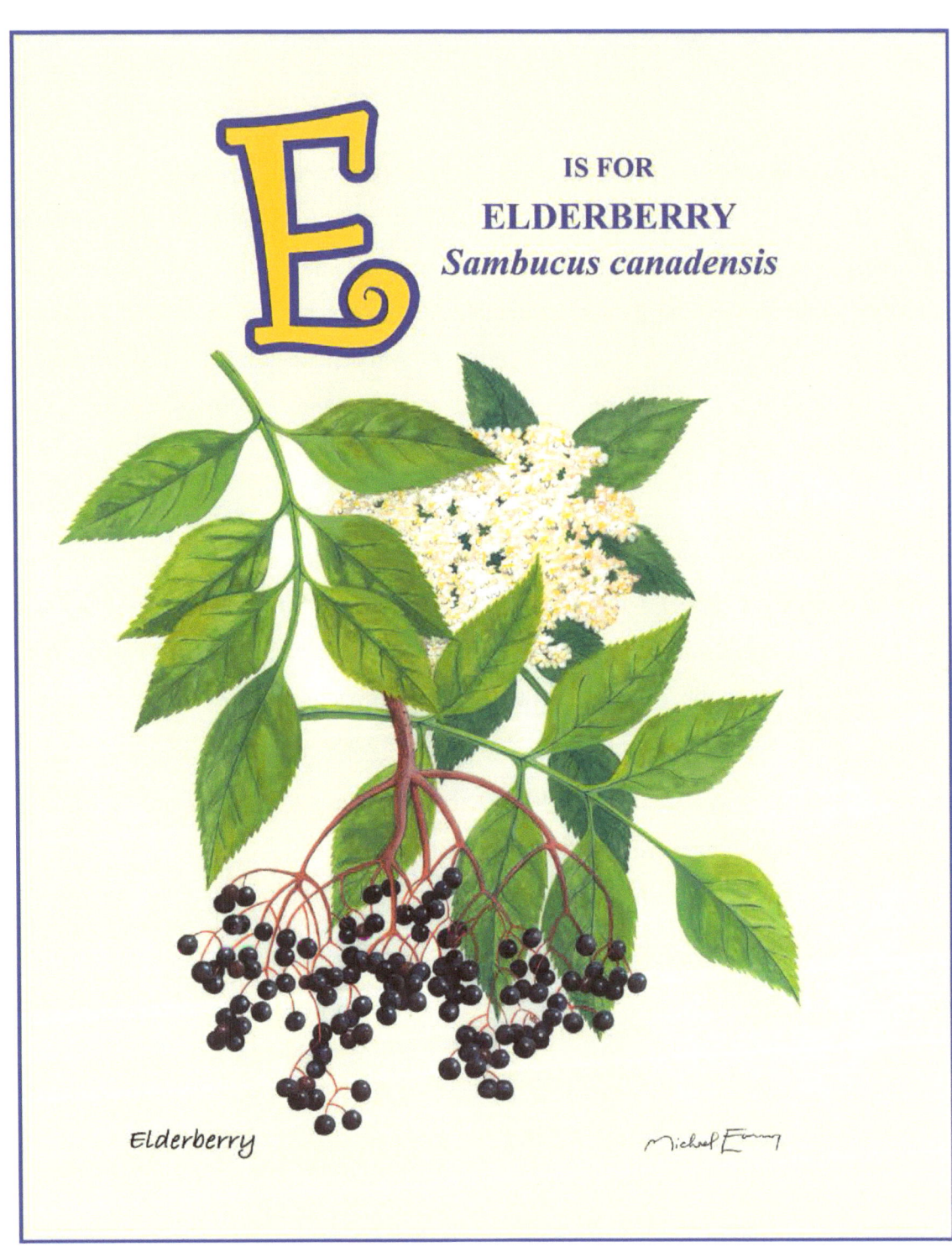

Elderberry is not only a lovely tree to behold when in flower or fruit, but delivers good eats in both stages. Don't pick the flower clusters, but carefully shake them into a bag or bucket; the undamaged fertilized ovaries left behind will go on to develop into fruit. The flowers can be mixed into a pancake batter. If you do pick the whole flower cluster they can be dipped in a tempura batter and fried. Though the blue-black berries are small they are easy to pick in their clusters. Make sure to remove any green berries and twigs, these are slightly toxic. Instead of picking the berries off, rubbing the clusters across a piece of half-inch mesh hardware cloth saves a lot of time. You are probably not going to enjoy the raw fruit; they are best cooked for jelly or jam, stewed, baked in a pie or dried and stored. The berries are a good source of important minerals and extremely rich in vitamins C and A. Enjoy elderflower fizz before it becomes elderflower champagne. If it becomes champagne, that needs to be drunk before the bottle explodes (usually in less than a year). Elderberry wine was a favorite of my grandmother who ascribed all kinds of healthful effects to it.

Cool fact: The soft pith inside the stem of the elderberry shrub is easily removed leaving a hollow tube that can be made into a whistle or, as when I was a kid, used as a peashooter.

What other wild plant starts with E?

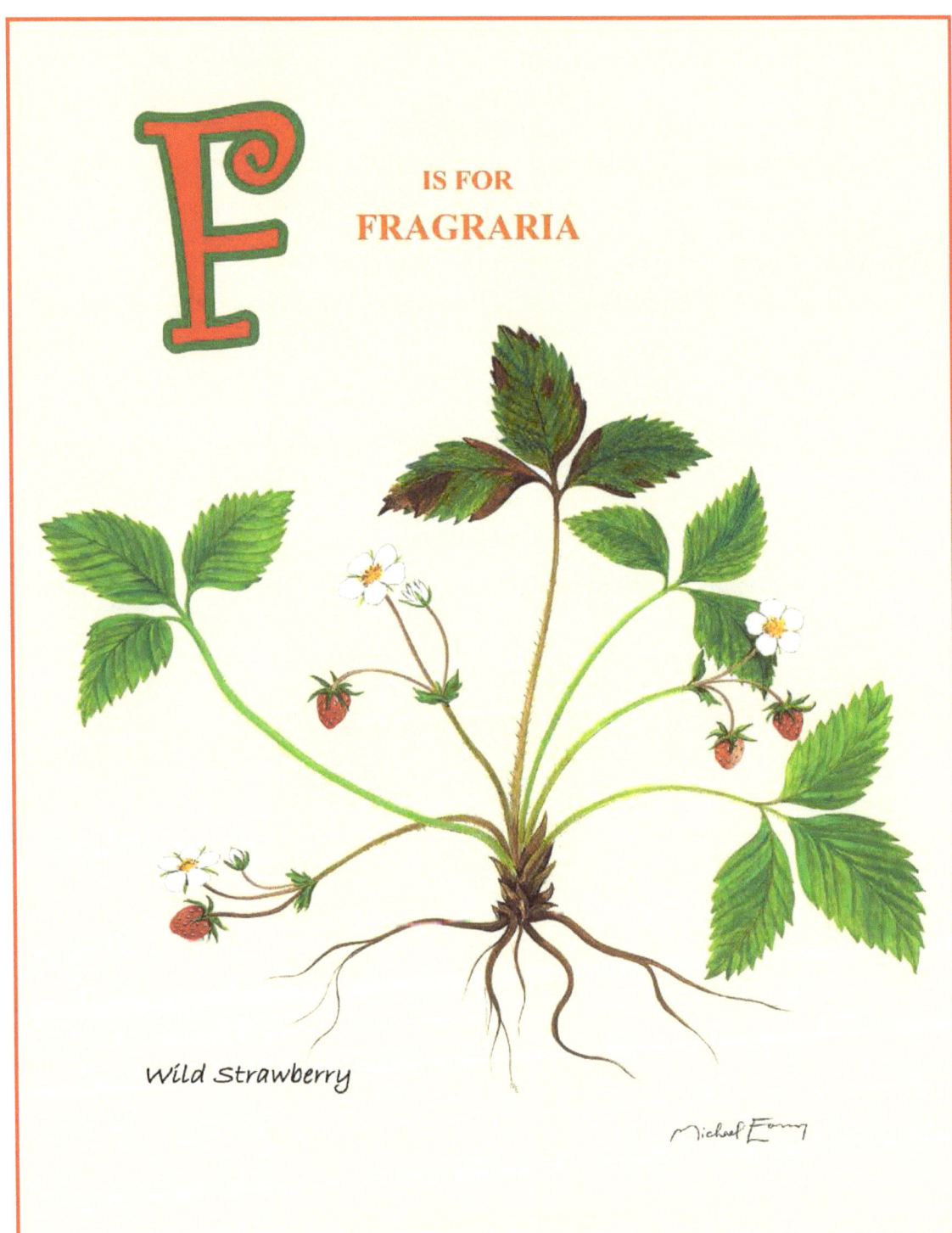

Fragaria is the genus, while *Rosaceae* is the family to which the strawberry belongs. If you want to impress your friends you can use those terms when ordering strawberry shortcake. Unfortunately, no one will know what you are talking about. Wild strawberries are so much more delicious than cultivated ones, you'll wish you could get them all the time, so take advantage when you can find them, the growing season is fairly short. If you wanted to cultivate them you can. A refreshing, vitamin-rich tea can be made from the fresh leaves. Keeping the brew overnight to drink cold the next day will deliver medicinal quantities of vitamin C. Or you can dry the leaves for later use. Make sure the leaves are thoroughly dry before storing them as wilted leaves develop a poison which disappears when they dry. If you are really hungry, the stalks and stems of the strawberry are also tasty.

Cool fact: By botanical definition the strawberry is a pseudofruit or accessory fruit; strictly speaking, the red part is a vegetable and the seeds are the fruit.

What other wild plant starts with F?

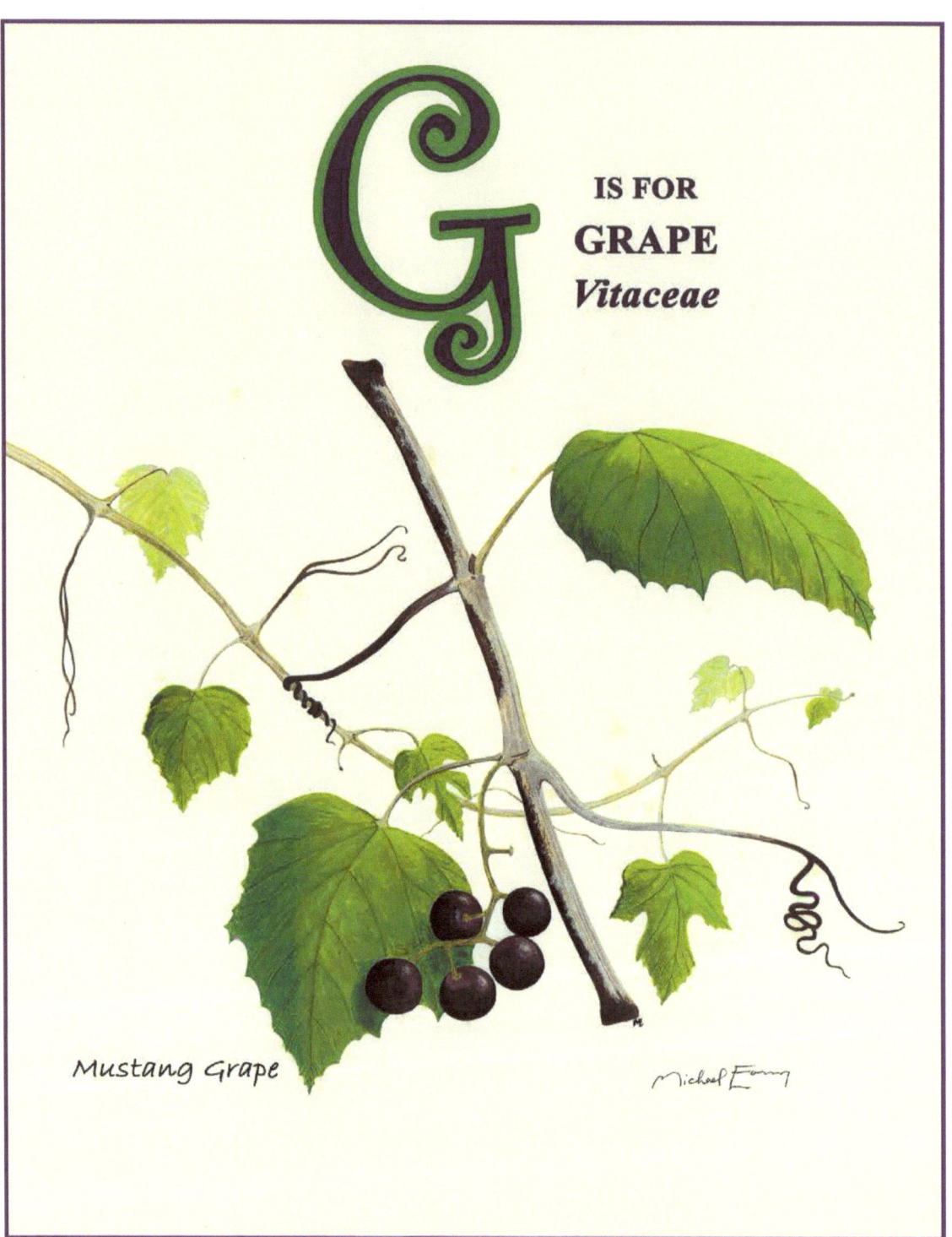

Grapes have been cultivated for more than 7000 years, mostly for wine. Even back in the days of the Roman Empire, Pliny the Elder (CE 23–CE 79), author and naturalist among other things, who wrote a many-volumed *natural history,* thought "It is extremely difficult to determine whether wine is more generally injurious in its effects or beneficial." A question still debated today.

Wild grapes, however – and at least half of the world's wild grapes are native to the American continent – have long been used for food by man, birds and beasts. In the spring the leaves and shoots can be eaten. Stuffed wild grape leaves will add a Mediterranean flavor to your meal. Though some wild grapes are sweeter than others, most are not so great straight from the vine, so adding sugar makes a big difference. Grape juice and grape jelly are quite easy to make. You can find recipes in some of the books listed in the bibliography, think conserves and pies too. Grapes are packed with vitamins, minerals and calories.

Cool fact: In 1860, when the deadly plant louse, Phylloxera, accidently imported from America, nearly decimated Europe's entire grape crop, wild grape rootstock, immune to the disease carried by the louse, were sent from Texas, surviving European grape vines were grafted onto them, saving the wine industry of France.

What other wild plant starts with G?

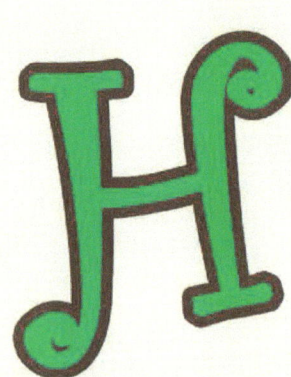

**IS FOR
HORSETAIL
*Equisetum arvense***

Horsetail

Michael Emry

Horsetail has been around for longer than just about any plant on the planet. Back in the Paleozoic era they grew to the size of trees (there is still a species in the tropics that grows to 30 feet). Also known as scouring rush, bottle brush, shave grass and pewterwort, it has been put to many uses for centuries, as some of its popular names indicate. Yet now it is considered a weed and a difficult one to get rid of.

Herbalists once prescribed it for a multitude of ills: anemia, abscesses, bleeding, bladder complaints, cuts, cancer—a veritable alphabet of disorders. One herbalist declared it, "Unique, irreplaceable, and invaluable." It can be used as a tea, a poultice, compress, gargle or a bath.

On the practical side, horsetail, because of its high silica content, was used to smooth and polish stone, metal and wood. It was used to clean the dishes in Europe at the same time as Native Americans were using it for the same purpose on this continent. So, although you can't eat it, horsetail will keep you healthy, it'll solve skin problems, cure sweaty feet and make your nails stronger.

Cool fact: Even if you pass on it, your garden plants might welcome a spray of the tea for its anti-mildew, anti-fungal benefits. Gentle and fast acting, it protects flowers, fruits and vegetables.

What other plants start with H?

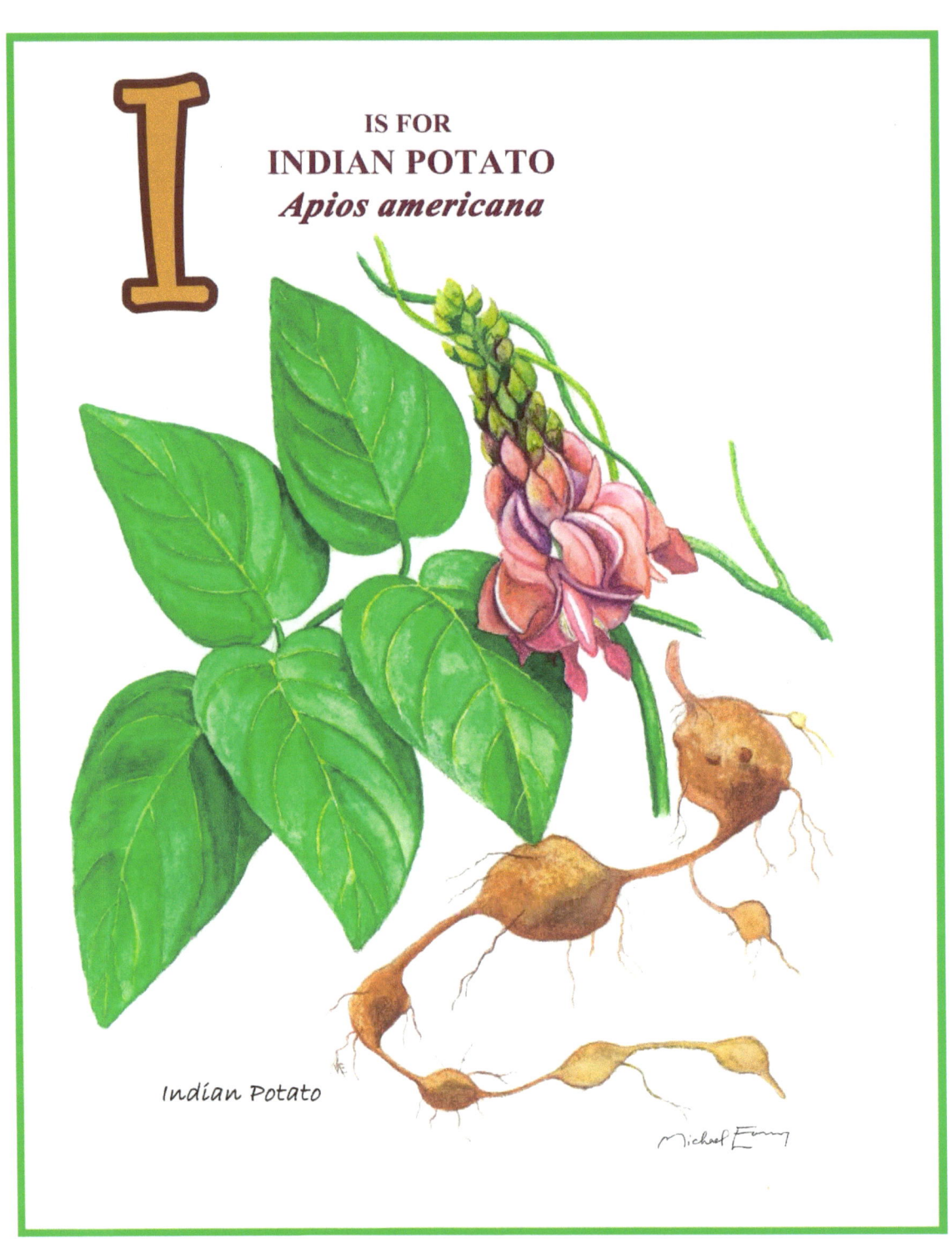

I IS FOR INDIAN POTATO
Apios americana

Indian Potato

Indian Potato is just one of the common names (also groundnut, wild bean, hopniss, bog potato, potato bean) for this member of the legume family. When a plant is known by many names it is usually an indication that it has been used by a wide variety of people over a long period of time. Massachusetts Indians introduced the Pilgrims to the plant which helped keep them alive through their first winters in the country. It grows widely in eastern North America, most readily along sandy river bottoms, in floodplains and wherever there is water and loose soil. The vine will twine up other plants but also spreads along the ground. While the fragrant flowers and the seeds can be eaten, it is the underground tubers, which can grow to the size of a regular baking potato, that are harvested for their protein. Some Native American tribes cultivated them as a staple, to be prepared and eaten in many different ways. Strung out along thin fibrous strands they will sometimes be found in great abundance requiring very little labor to extract them from the ground.

Cool fact: If there's any truth to the story, it is very likely that this was the potato that Sir Walter Raleigh (1552-1618) carried back to England and not the South American variety that we know as the potato today. Sir Walter tried unsuccessfully to establish Colonies in America for Queen Elizabeth the First. He named Virginia for her. Besides the potato, he introduced tobacco to Europe.

What other plant starts with I?

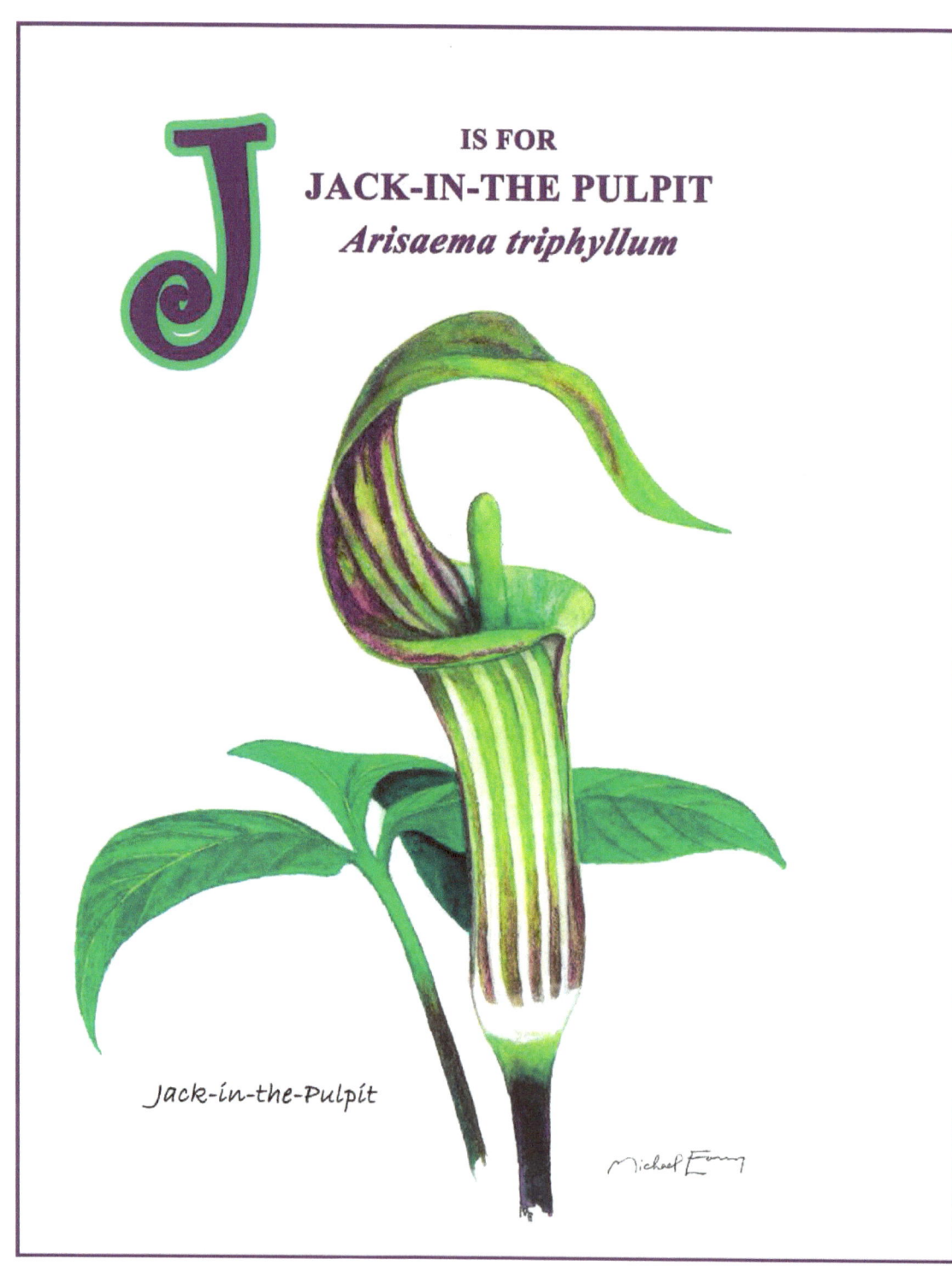

Jack-in-the-Pulpit gets its name from its resemblance to certain old-timey church pulpits where there is a canopy over the enclosed pulpit and the stalk, or spadix, looks like the vicar standing there. It is also called Indian turnip, a name that comes from the fact that Native Americans used the turnip-shaped root or corm for food and medicine. You may not want to mess with it since it is toxic fresh and should *never* be eaten that way. However, like so many things, mankind found a way to make it edible. I'm quoting Euell Gibbons here as he tried it and found that it had to be thoroughly dried, and I do mean thoroughly, like, five months! The thinly sliced chips then had an excellent flavor and could be roasted to eat like potato chips. Crumbled and boiled for 10 minutes to make a cereal, or ground into a flour to mix half and half with wheat flour or some other flour if you're avoiding gluten (the Indian potato has none); it can be made into bread or cakes, etc. You can find a recipe in Euell Gibbons' book, "Stalking the Healthful Herbs." As he says there, he enjoys eating it, and any health benefits, of which there are said to be many, are a bonus.

Cool fact: The plant starts as a male, but after two years, if it is growing in poor soil, it becomes female, flowers and develops shiny red berries which, like the fresh root, will burn your mouth and could do more harm if swallowed. If the now-female plant receives a shock (don't step on it!) it may turn back to male again (it's hermaphroditic).

What other plant starts with J?

K

IS FOR
KNIGHT'S MILFOIL
Achillea millefolium

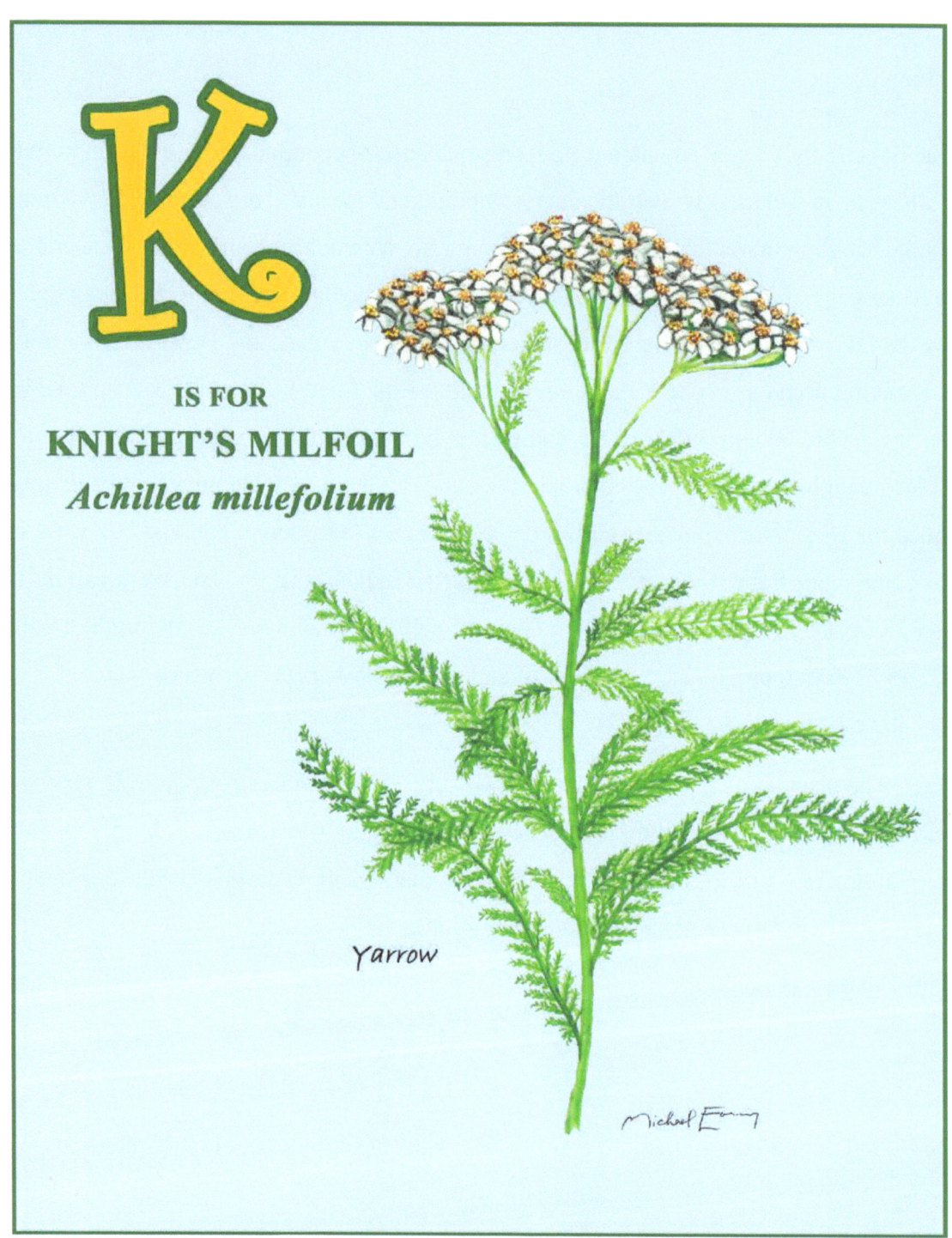

Yarrow

Knight's Milfoil is just one of the many names for yarrow; nosebleed, carpenter's weed, devil's plaything and soldier's woundwort are some of the others. Like many of our weeds, yarrow was brought to this country by people who had a need for it and it went wild. Raw, yarrow is rather bitter, but finely chopped leaves can be added to soups and salads; don't overdo it, there is some concern about the toxins it contains.

Yarrow tea is good for internal and external problems; rheumatism, toothache, earache, blackheads, oily hair—just some targets once claimed for this "all heal" weed. In the past it was used to stop bleeding, but was also said to be able to both staunch a nosebleed, or start one, depending on what you want.

An old incantation went: "Yarroway, yarroway, bear a white blow, if my love loves me, my nose will bleed now".

Cool fact: Yarrow stalks are used in throwing the I Ching, the ancient Chinese divination system. "Take 50 straight, smooth sticks, 7 to 13 inches long. Set one aside, now take the 49 remaining, divide into two bunches, set down the bunch in your right hand. Take one stalk from the right hand pile, place it between the fourth and little finger . . ." Well, it gets a little complicated. You may want to use the three-coin method instead. But if you have any questions, ask the I Ching.

What other wild plants start with the letter K?

L
IS FOR
LAMB'S QUARTERS
Chenopodium album

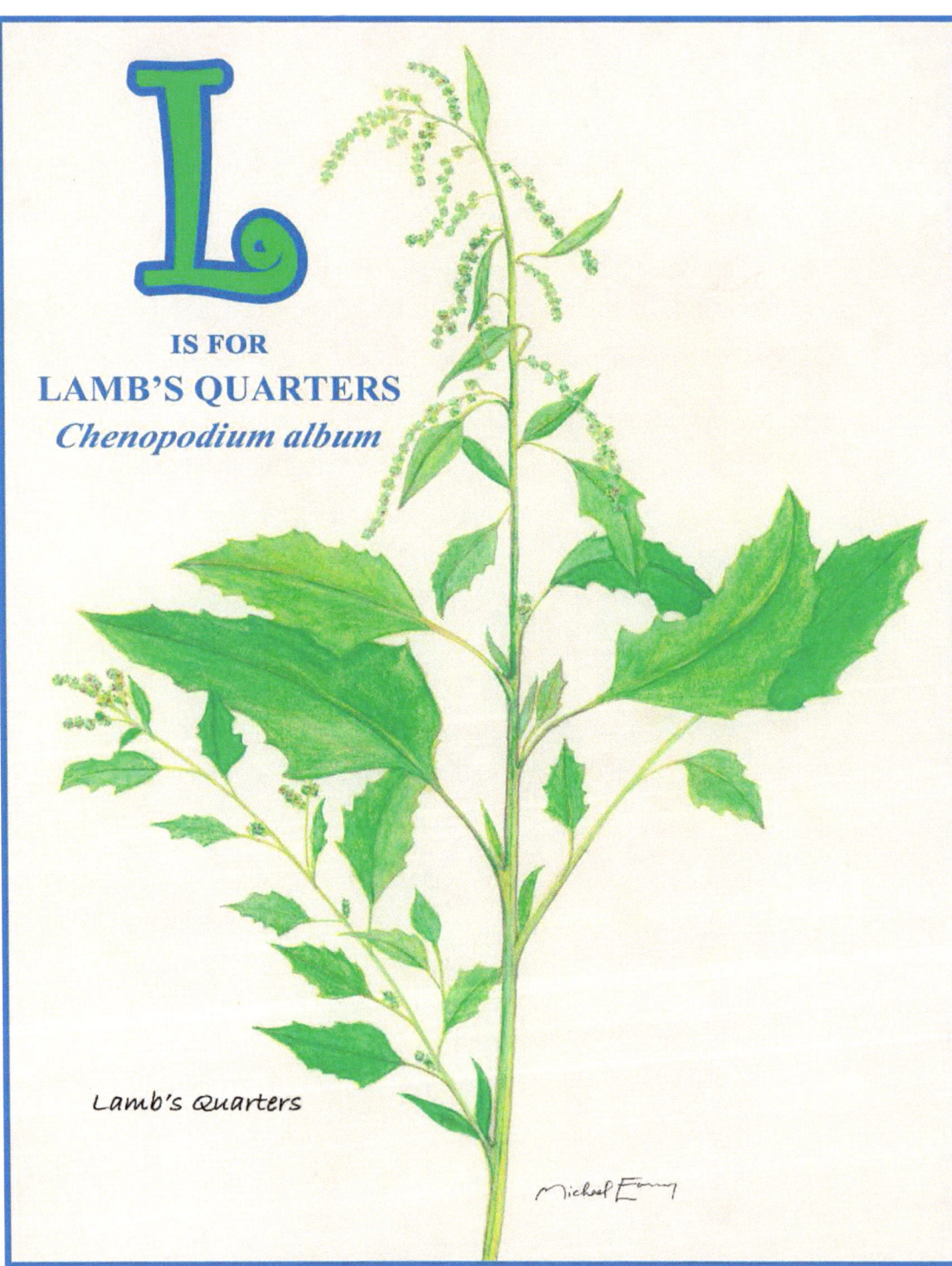

Lamb's Quarters

Lamb's quarters (goosefoot, pigweed, wild spinach, fat hen) is another weed so common that no one notices it. It can grow in the worst of soil. My first encounter with it was in Venice, California, where I saw a five-foot plant growing out of a crack in the sidewalk. But it really enjoys rich soil; its long taproot can reach lower than many other plants. By releasing nutrients from the depths it helps improve the soil and benefits those plants with shorter roots. Related to spinach, it is actually richer in vitamin C and A, is a good source of the same minerals found in spinach and is the richest source of calcium of any leafy green vegetable. So you don't have to eat your spinach—as long as you eat lamb's quarters! When it is little the entire plant can be eaten; as it grows, just strip the leaves off that you are going to eat. If you get to really liking it, it is possible to blanch and freeze baggies of them for the winter. The seeds are easily gathered to use like chia seeds or cooked like a cereal. They can be ground and mixed with flour for pancakes, muffins or rolls. Try them in cornbread.

That common name, fat hen? That's because chickens love it and it helps produce tender meat and eggs with dark yolks. A wide variety of birds and animals, from sparrows to chipmunks, eat the seeds.

Cool fact: Nearly 7500 seeds have been counted on a single plant! Wait, was that 6000 or 7000? Better start over. One, two, three. . .

What other plant starts with L?

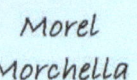

M

IS FOR

MUSHROOM

Morel
Morchella

Mushrooms, toadstools, these are two names often used to distinguish edible from poisonous fungi but, in fact, mushrooms and toadstools are the same thing. You don't have to be any more afraid of mushrooms than the other plants you'll find in the wild. Luckily some of the most delicious and highly prized are easy to distinguish from their inedible or poisonous counterparts. If you are interested in eating mushrooms get a good guide, someone knowledgeable and/or a good book. Learn to identify the edible ones first, like the common meadow mushroom, chanterelles, boletes and morels. There are false chanterelles and morels, but many of the false versions are edible too. Some boletes are not so tasty but the most common ones are. The amanitas are the family to be wary of, they can kill, yet the *Amanita caesarea* is one of the most highly sought edibles there is. The mushroom you pick is the flower or fruiting body of the mycelium growing underground. When gathering them, cut the stem; pulling the mushroom out could break the mother plant, the mycelium.

Cool fact: As of August 2014, the largest living organism on earth is the mycelium of an armillaria or honey mushroom growing in the Malheur National Forest in Oregon. It is estimated to be 2400 years old and stretches 3.5 miles across. Unfortunately, the mycelium lives off and eventually kills, trees. In the process it emits bright flashes, known as foxfire light.

What other plant starts with M?

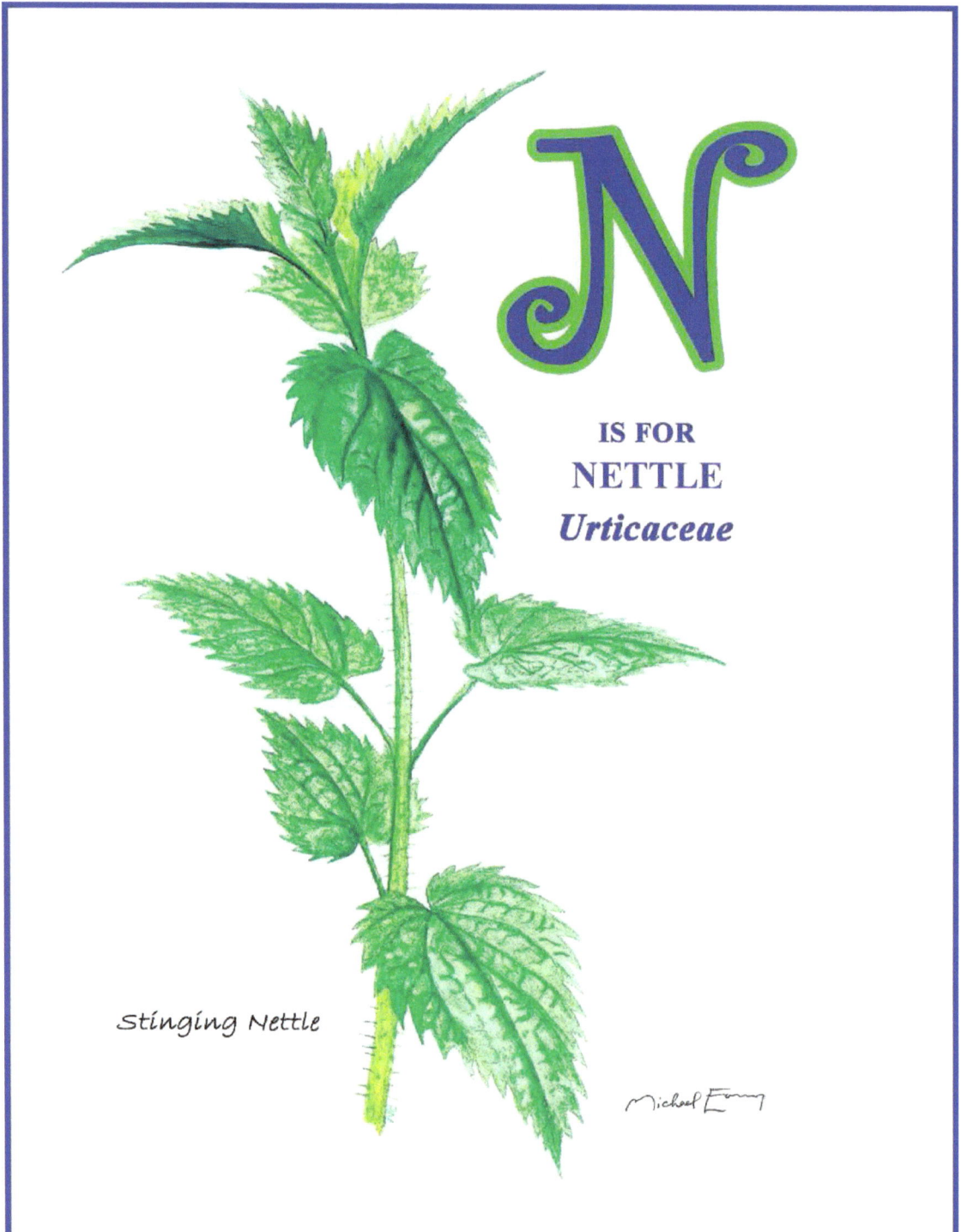

Nettles (stinging nettle, slender nettle, great, and dwarf nettle) are shunned by most people: they're afraid of getting stung, with good reason, it does itch. The juice from a leaf of dock or aloe vera will ease the pain. Like so many other weeds, nettles have been used by so many people all over the world for so many things it's amazing that now so few people know anything about them. They are great to eat; pick them when they are around knee high, snap or snip the stem about six inches down and head for the kitchen.

Omelettes to soups and salads, tea and even beer can be made. The nettle has been used for making clothing and many other textiles, from fine bed linen to sail cloth. As medicine, it has had too many applications to list here. No doubt it's high concentration of vitamins C and D and numerous minerals contribute to its healing powers. It's good as a face pack, an after-shampoo rinse and is said to stimulate hair growth. Farmers once harvested nettles; dried, it was fed to the barnyard animals. The dried seeds and powdered leaves kept their chickens healthy and increased their egg production.

Cool fact: What came first, nettle or net? Both words have similar roots and meaning: 'to twist, knot'; 'something knotted'. Fishing nets were once made with nettle fiber – the long fibers are extracted from the stem of the plant and woven. In Asia, bags made of nettle netting are still made for carrying large loads, or the nettles one has picked for dinner.

What other plant starts with N?

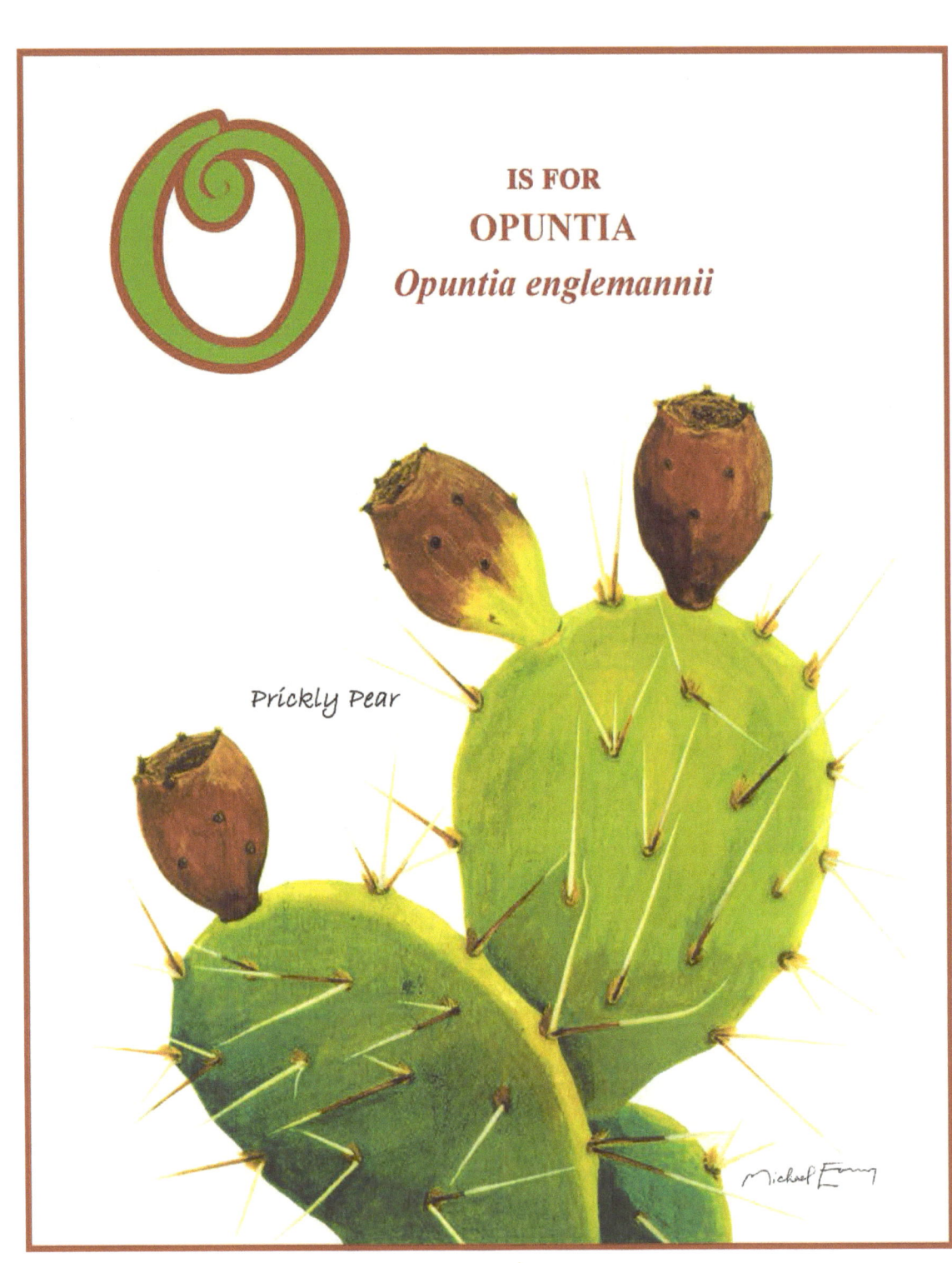

O IS FOR
OPUNTIA
Opuntia englemannii

Prickly Pear

Opuntia engelmannii, the prickly pear, is the cactus that most commonly comes to mind since, unlike some others, it has spread over large areas of land, especially those over-grazed by cattle or goats. The prickly pear has splendid flowers, showy fruit and altogether, of all the cacti, provides the most edible parts. There are many other cacti, most of which have some edible parts (the strawberry cactus has fruit that actually tastes like strawberries). The flat, roundish pads, the nopals, are harvested when young before developing the spines that protect it from foraging animals and will no doubt prick you however hard you try to avoid it. In Mexico you will see ladies sitting in the market scraping them clean, ready to make *nopalitos y huevos* or any number of dishes. Then there are the tunas, the fruit (which is eaten green or ripe) that grow along the edge of the nopal. I should say that the flowers can be eaten, but then there will be no tunas. Bright red, the ripe tunas provide so much vitamin C that you can feel it doing you good when you drink a glass of the juice.

Cool fact: The small white woolly webs that often appear on the pads contain a tiny insect that when squeezed, spurt out a bright red dye. In my dad's bake house there was a bottle containing a red liquid used to add color to cakes. It was called cochineal. It was only many years later I learned that the cochineal insect from the cactus provided that coloring agent.

What other plant begins with O?

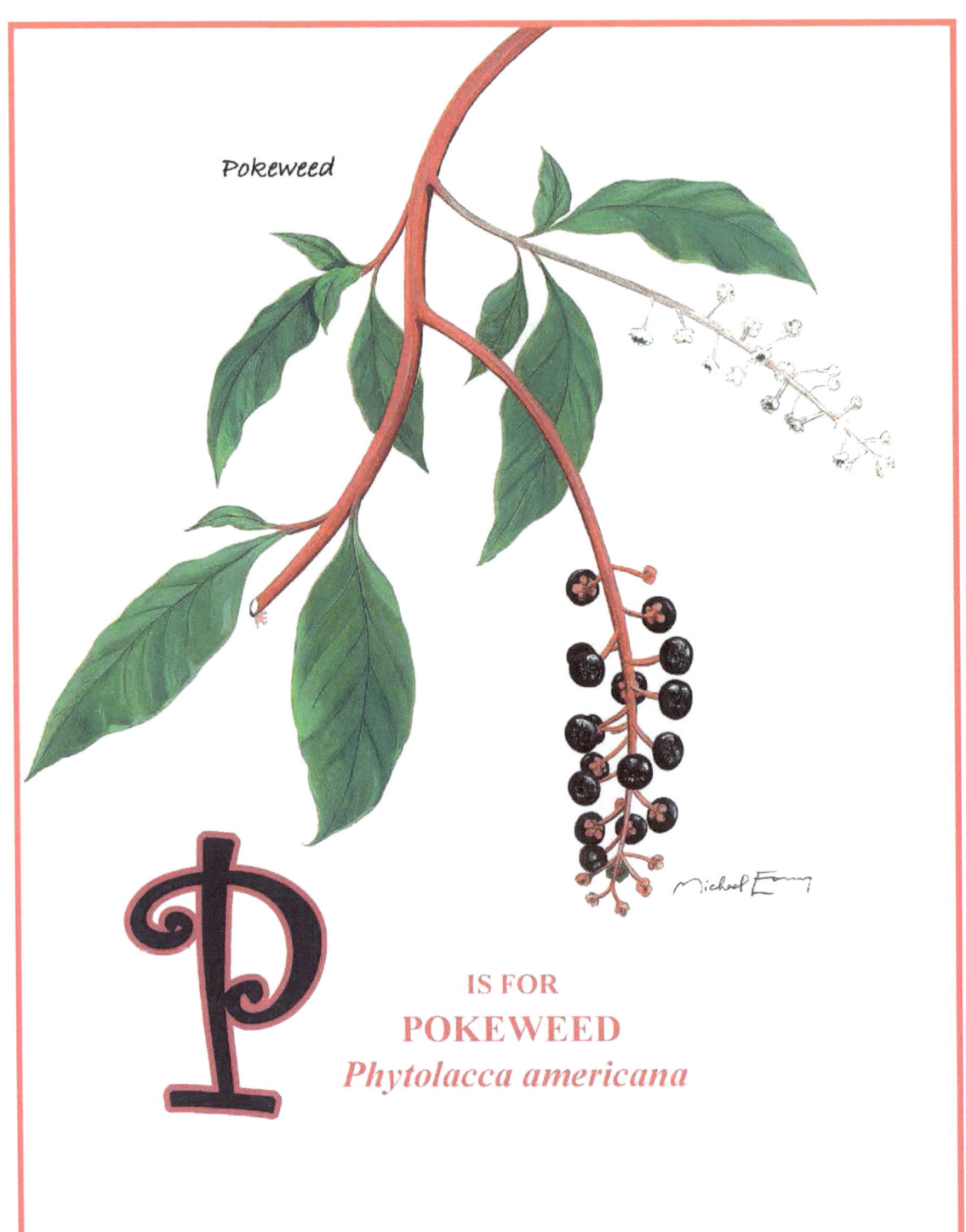

Pokeweed (coakum, chongras, american nightshade) is another of those deadly poisonous plants that people figured out how to eat. It is generally agreed that the young plant, not more than six to eight inches high, can be gathered, boiled once, twice or three times, changing the water each time and, with the addition of salt and pepper and a little oil, makes the most delicious potherb of all potherbs. The stems, so long as they are not red, can be peeled and fried like okra. It should never be eaten raw; the berries are toxic, the root is toxic and older parts of the plant are toxic, causing severe stomach problems and even death. Old-timers who have eaten the plant all their lives scoff at such concerns, saying they've eaten parts of the plant considered toxic without any ill effects, that they pop a couple of berries every day for their arthritis. The fact is, those parts are known to be poisonous, so why take chances? At the same time it is true the seeds, stems and roots are used in folk medicine. A half cup of those boiled tender leaves provide 90% of the daily requirement of vitamin A, 60% of vitamin C, 8% calcium and 6% iron, plus fiber.

Cool fact: Researchers at Wake Forest University's Center for Nanotechnology and Molecular Materials applied poke juice to fiber-based solar panels. They found that the pigment or dye helped the cells' fibers to capture more sunlight and change it into power. (See www.inhabitat.com, 4/30/10).

What other plant starts with P?

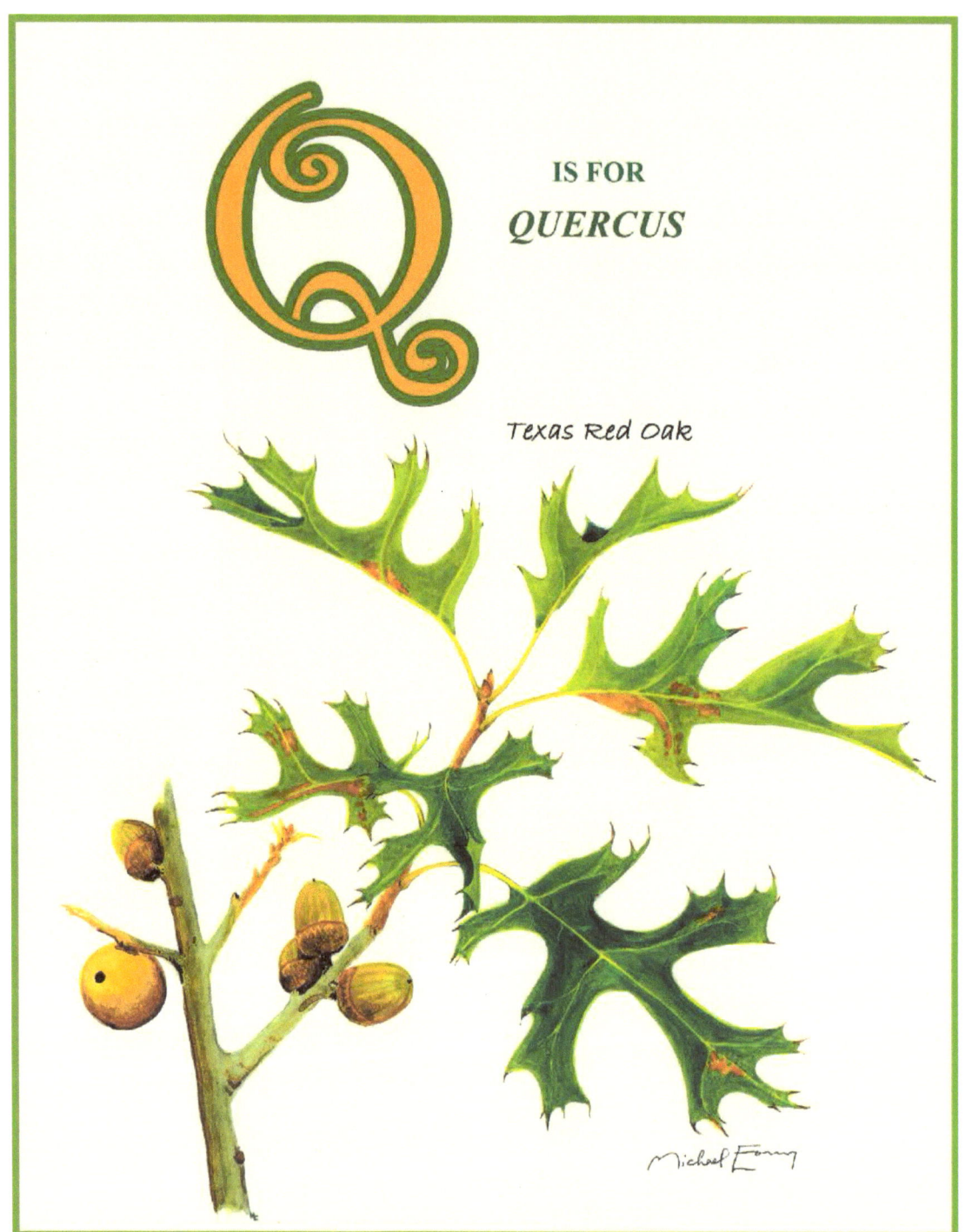

Quercus, the mighty oak, provided a staple food for any number of creatures, including humans, for thousands of years. Although some acorns are low enough in tannin to be eaten raw, most are not. Early man, both here and abroad, learned how to remove the tannin from the acorns: submerging them in a running stream will remove it overnight. Shelled, the acorns were generally ground into flour for baking, or added to soup. Roasted acorns have also been ground and used as a coffee substitute. Various parts of the tree have been used medicinally; the bark is used for tanning skins and in dye making. Above all, perhaps, the oak is most valued for its wood. Extremely hard and resistant to rot, it became the symbol of strength and endurance. In many countries and cultures the oak has been revered as the seventh and chief of the seven great trees in the tree alphabet calendar; it ruled supreme. The oak's human representative, the Oak King, was worshipped as the god who ruled the waxing year, dying and being reborn each winter solstice. Early Christian churches were built in sacred oak groves, appropriating to themselves the inherent holiness of the place. Harry Potter fans know that a magic wand of oak is the best.

Cool fact: Built in 1765, Admiral Lord Nelson's ship, HMS Victory, required about 6000 mature oak trees, clearing one hundred acres of oak forest. The largest trees were used for the 30-foot high stern post; seven trees were needed for each of the ship's three masts and bowsprit.

What other tree begins with Q?

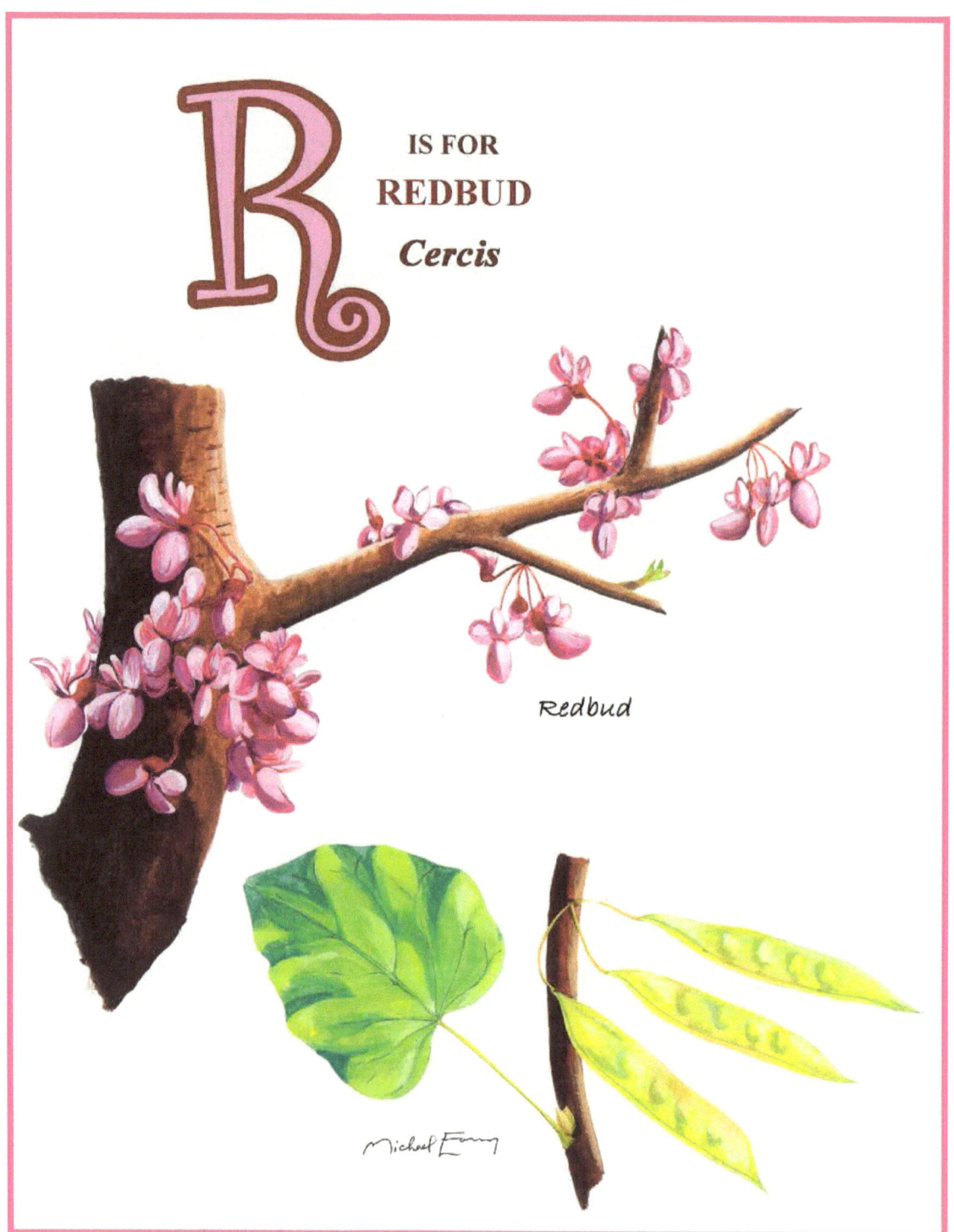

Redbud trees give the spirit a lift when, on a cold, overcast winter's day, one catches a dash of bright magenta pink against the grey and black background of trees—the redbud is in flower! But it has more to offer. Those flowers can be eaten raw, tossed in a salad, added to pancakes, fried or pickled. The redbud, also known as the Judas tree, is in the legume family so when the pods are young they can be cooked the same way as peas. Later yet, the seeds can be roasted and eaten. In southern Appalachia the tree is known as spicewood; the green twigs are used to season venison or other wild game dishes. Native Americans boiled the bark for a tea to relieve whooping cough, while the roots and bark were used for fever and congestion. Some birds, squirrels and whitetail deer partake of the tree's various parts, and a yellow dye can be made from it too. In Texas it rarely grows to any great size, but it puts on that burst of color just when it's needed. The name Judas tree came about through a misunderstanding of the Latin name, *Arbor judea*, tree of Judea. It grew abundantly around Jerusalem; this led to it being called Judas tree and the legend that Judas Iscariot hung himself from it.

Cool fact: You can justify having that bowl of ice cream if you throw in some redbud flowers; not only do they add a distinctive color, they are really high in vitamin C. How about that, healthy ice cream!

What other plants start with R?

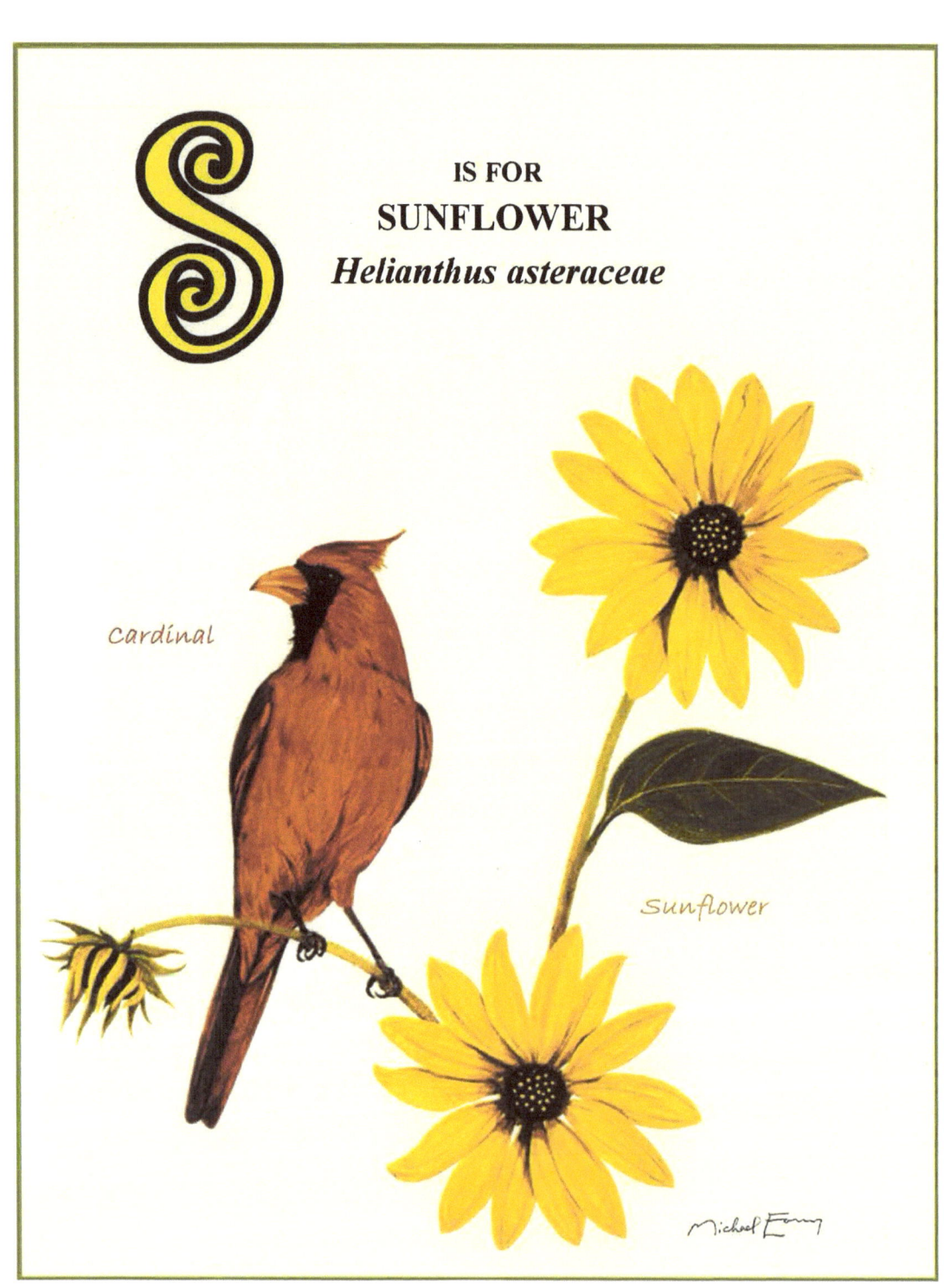

Sunflowers (mirasol, girasol) belong to a large family; in fact, the largest flowering plant family in the world. As you can imagine, many of them look alike though they may vary greatly in size. Many are responsible for what we call 'hay fever' and many are valuable agricultural crops, including the plant that's actually called the sunflower. Native Americans developed giant sunflowers long before Europeans came to this country. The sunflower is the only major crop that originated in what is now the USA, though the commercially grown sunflower seeds and oil you buy in the store may be from cultivars developed in Russia.

You can eat more than just the seeds (which are a good source of protein, vitamins and minerals) from the wild sunflowers that grow so abundantly. The tiny unopened flower buds are tasty and the Maximilian sunflower has rootlets that, like the Jerusalem artichoke to which it is related, can be eaten raw, roasted or boiled. Dyes can be obtained from the flowers and roots. A wide variety of birds eat the seeds. The cardinal must have flown in from my other book, "The A to Z Book of Birds".

Cool fact: The Maximilian sunflower is named for Prince Maximilian, the German explorer, ethnologist and naturalist. While in North America he and his companion, the painter Karl Bodmer, recorded in writing and watercolors much about the Indian people and collected botanical and zoological specimens. Unfortunately, many of these were lost in a fire aboard the ship carrying them back to Germany.

What other plants start with S?

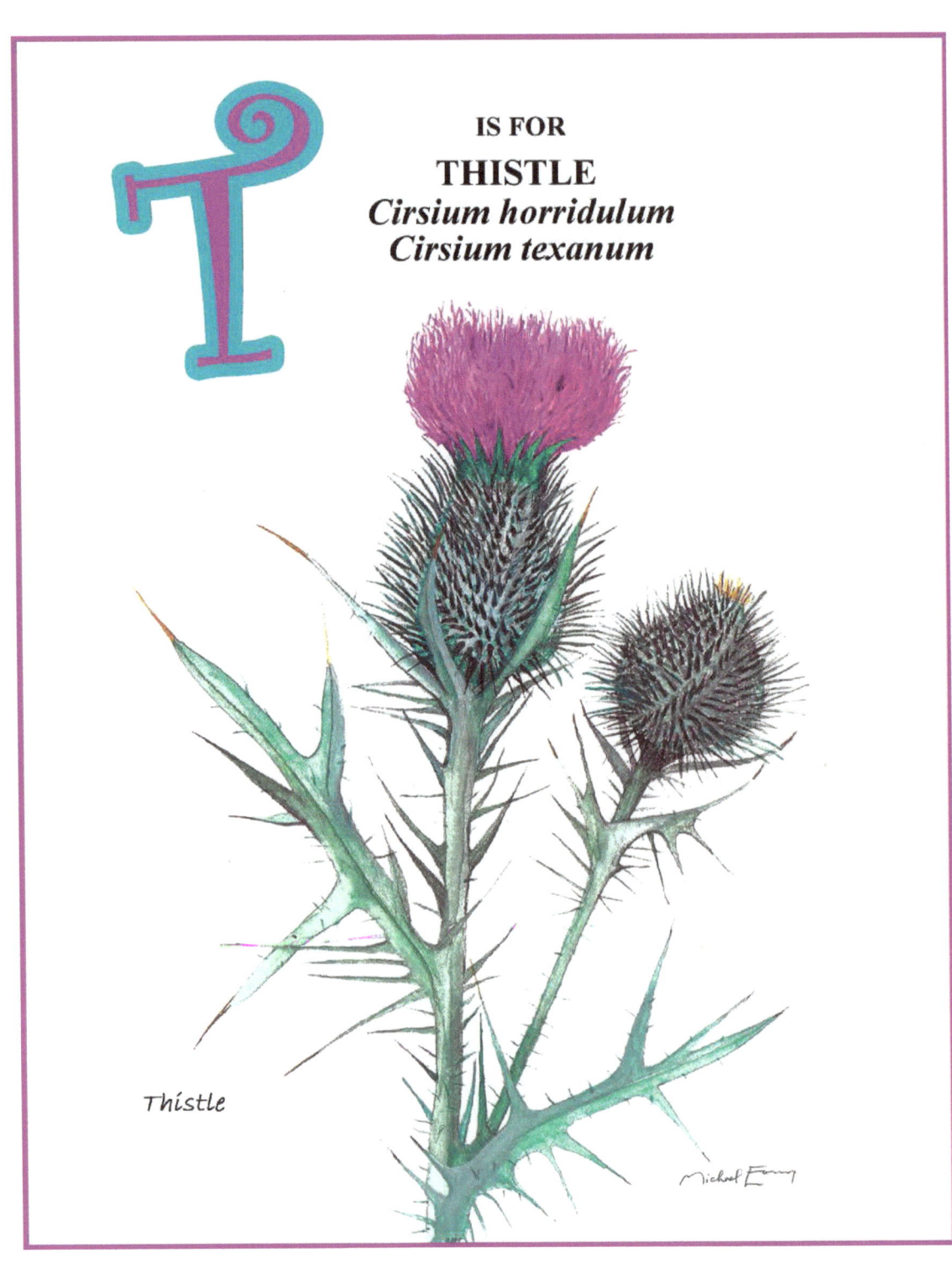

T IS FOR **THISTLE**
Cirsium horridulum
Cirsium texanum

Thistle

Thistles (the armored knight) are probably next in line to dandelions in the weed ranking; *horridulum* sounds bad too, doesn't it? One look and you can't think of any reason to eat it. But you would be surprised. You will need stout gloves to gather them and to hold the leaves while you clip off the spines. Stick with it though because they provide some of the best cooked and salad greens, yes, salad greens!

From fall to early spring gather the large basal leaves, and dig up the taproot as this can be added raw to a salad too. In the early spring, before the flowers open, the young stalks, without the spines and outer layer, give you a tender vegetable to eat raw or steamed. The flower buds, well before they open, can also be cooked and eaten. Butterflies and bees visit the flowers to sup and birds dine on the seeds. It is also used medicinally. The milk thistle has been used for some 2000 years for gallbladder and liver diseases.

Cool fact: The thistle has been the symbol of Scotland for hundreds of years: ever since a member of an invading force of Norsemen, having sailed across from Norway to the Scottish coast, stepped on some thistles and his screams of agony alerted the Scots, enabling them to defend their country and defeat the invaders. In 1540 King James V established a knighthood called the Order of the Thistle.

What other plant starts with T?

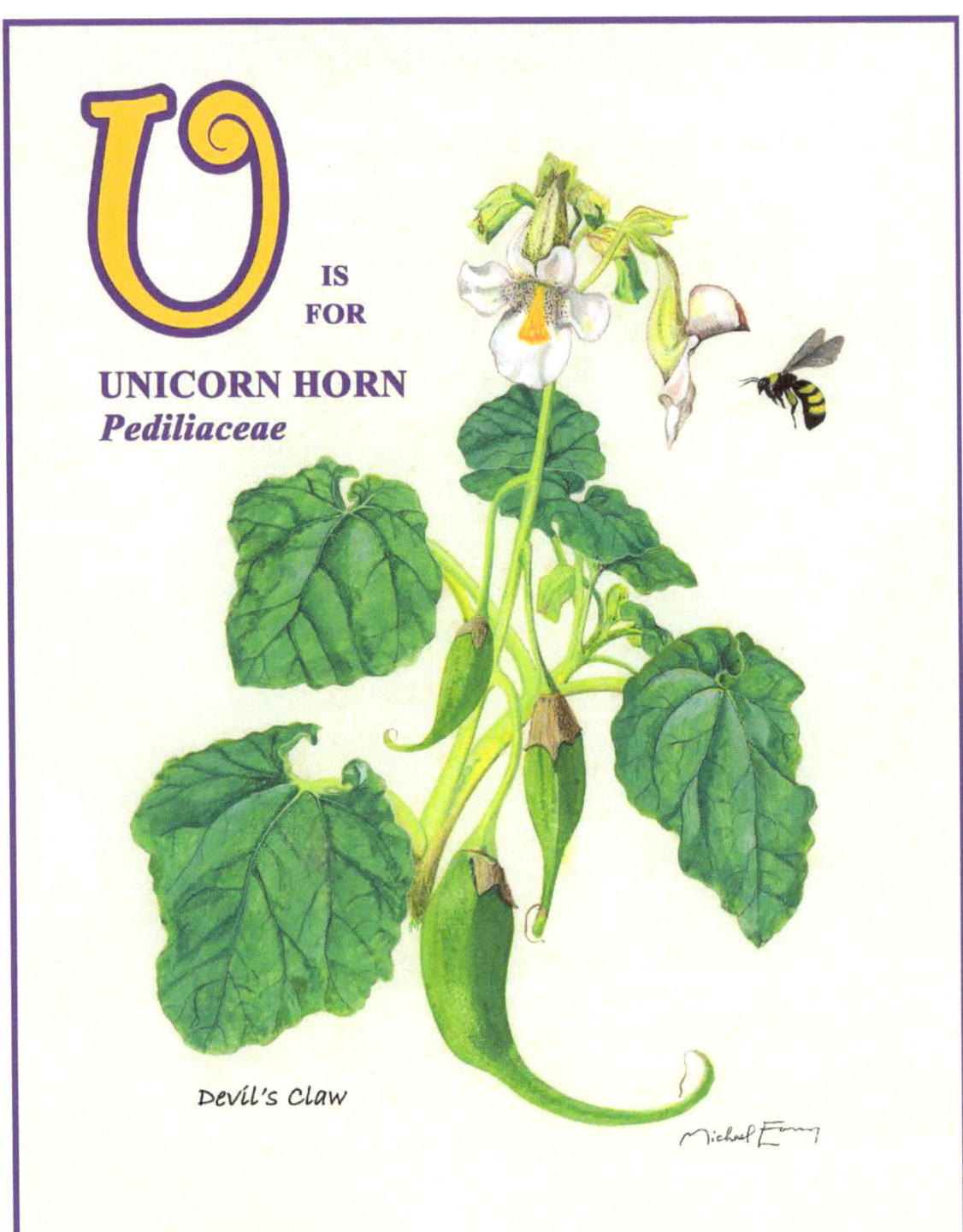

U IS FOR
UNICORN HORN
Pediliaceae

Devil's Claw

Unicorn plants are very distinctive when the dry seed pods have opened and the two halves of the split pod form the curving claws that are responsible for its several names (devil's claw, ram's horn, uña de gato, torito). Unfortunately, this is the time when about the only thing you can use it for is to hang up your potholders or as decoration. In early summer the young tender pods, less than two inches long, when washed and the sticky hairs brushed off, can be boiled or substituted for okra in gumbo. They are also, apparently, good pickled. If you get to the ripe pods before they open, the seeds are very tasty; immature they can be eaten, coat and all, otherwise remove the seed coat and enjoy them fresh, roasted or ground to a meal that can be added to flour. We are told that the Tarahumara Indians, the famous runners, cook the leaves of uña de gato (that's cat's claw, if your Spanish is not so good) in with beans.

Cool fact: *Proboscidea louisianica* (unicorn plant, devil's claw, ram's horn, uña de gato, torito) we are now told belongs not in the *Martyniaceae* family, but in *Pediliaceae* (sesame) family. Does that mean unicorns do exist or that they don't exist?

N.B. Carl Linnaeus (1707-78) created a system for classifying plants, building on earlier attempts. New plants and new knowledge mean the system is always being tweaked.

What other plants start with U?

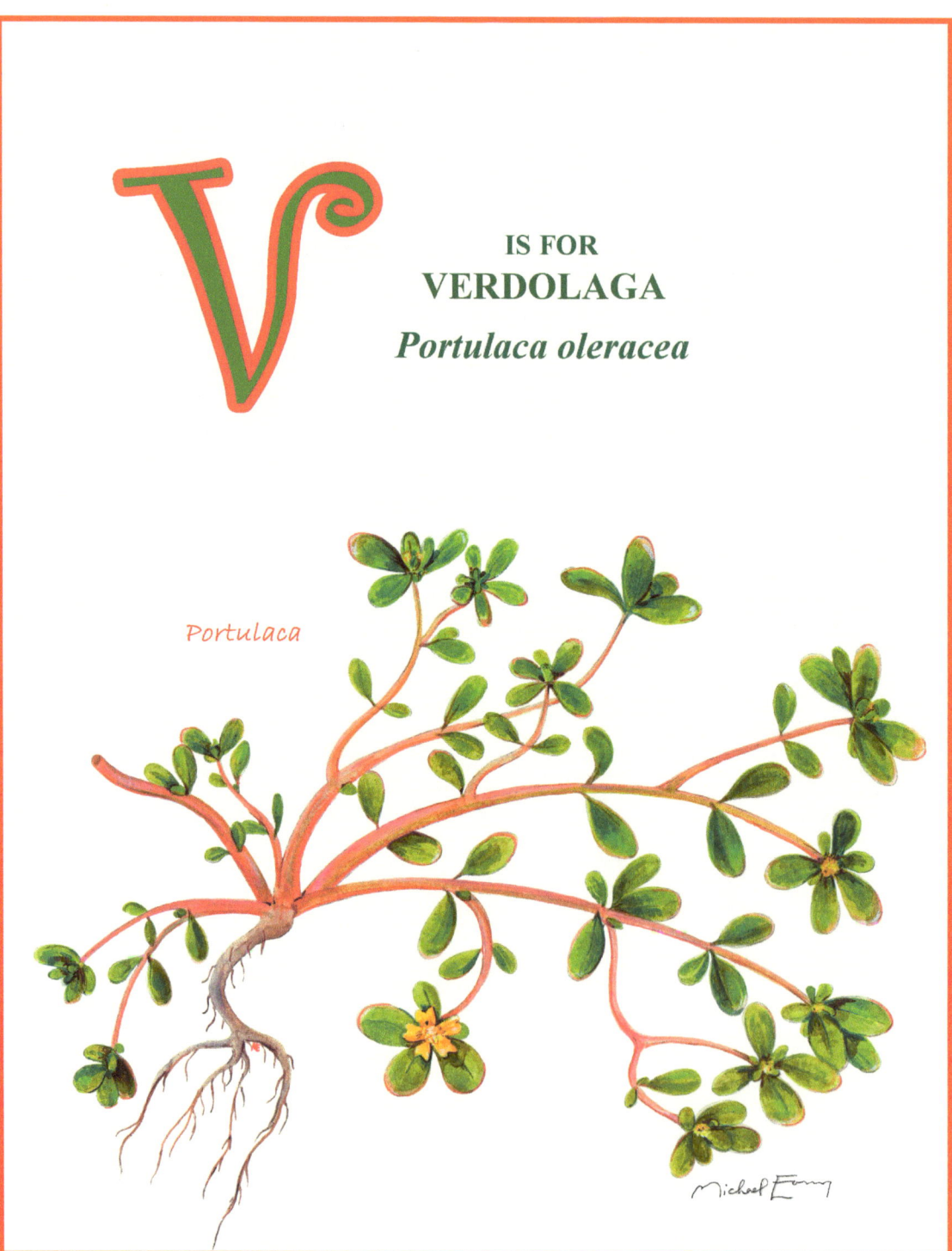

V IS FOR VERDOLAGA
Portulaca oleracea

Portulaca

Verdolaga is another of those weeds that are so below the radar that scarcely anyone will notice it or could tell you how beneficial a plant it is. Better known, if known at all, as purslane and portulaca, it is usually pulled up and thrown away if in a garden bed, but this lowly plant has more iron than any plant other than parsley, is high in vitamins A and C and good amounts of riboflavins, while being low in calories. The stems, with leaves intact, can be chopped and thrown in with other salad greens or, with olive oil and lime juice, eaten on its own. The stems can get quite thick, at which time they can be pickled. Like okra, it is mucilaginous; its juice gives body to soups and stews. After the little yellow flowers fade in late summer, you can harvest the tiny seeds and they can be ground and mixed with flour for baking. I have eaten it in New Mexico and old Mexico, from one mile high to sea level; it is everywhere. Native to Persia, Arabs introduced it to Europe in the 15th century and the early colonialists brought it to America. It can supply healthy greens all summer long.

Cool fact: In 1906 Mahatma Gandhi adopted his method of *satyagraha* (devotion to truth) or non-violent protest. Later, during his campaign to help the people of India end British rule, he encouraged self-sufficiency which included eating native weeds. Purslane, loaded with omega-3 fatty acids, was one weed he highly recommended.

What other plants start with V?

W IS FOR WATER HYACINTH
Eichhornia crassipes

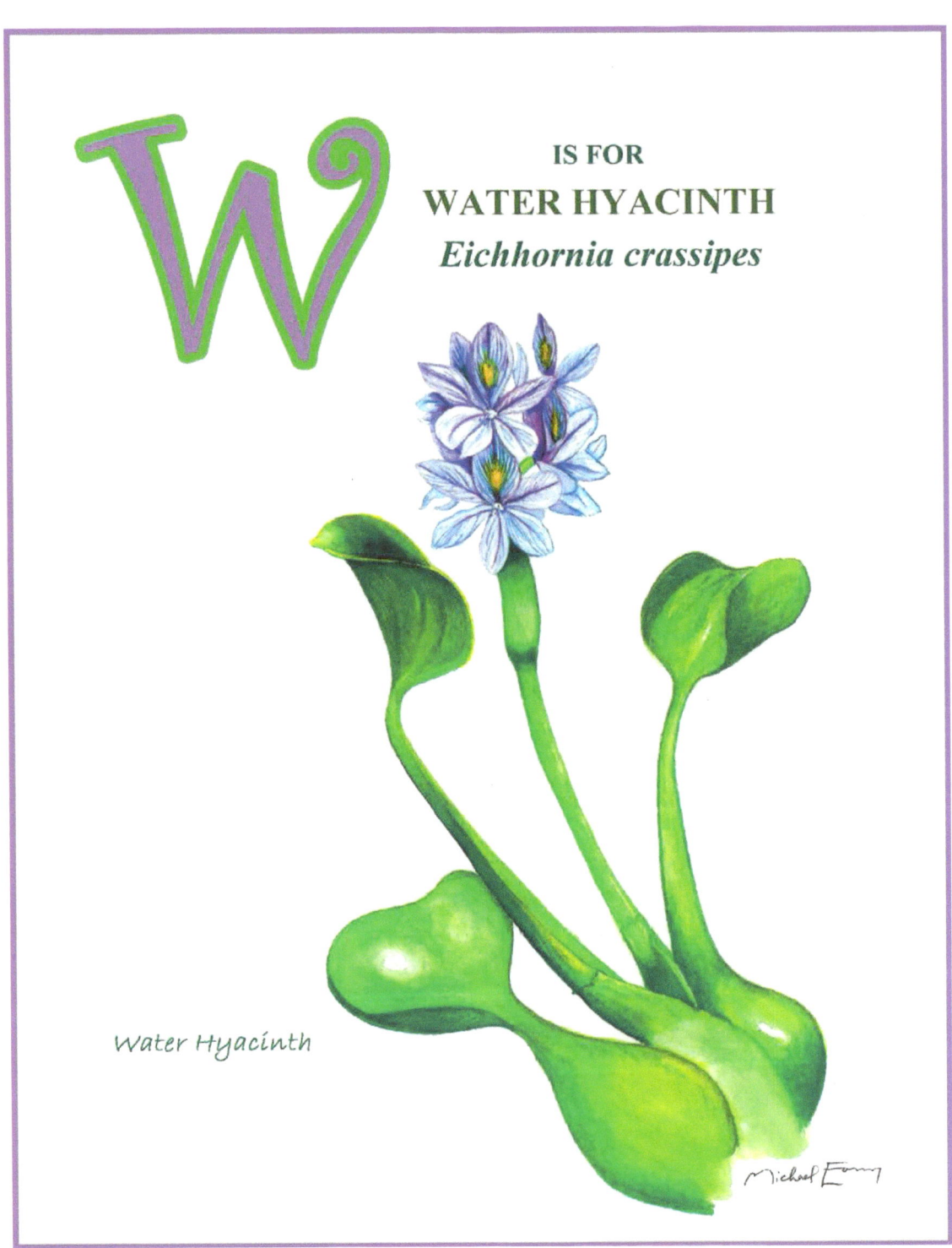

Water Hyacinth

Water hyacinth. Pretty, isn't it? A noxious weed, nevertheless. Since it was taken from its native Brazil to the USA in 1884 it has spread around the world, clogging rivers and streams, blocking sunlight from lakes and ponds, causing the death of fish and other aquatic life. Tearing them out won't work; the spongy bladder at the end of each leaf means they can float away and root again. And anyway, they leave seeds and roots behind that in short order replace those that were eliminated. Millions of dollars have been spent to eradicate it, without success. Here's the good news though, water hyacinth is edible. Boiled or steamed the young plants taste similar to asparagus. A flour rich in vitamins, minerals, protein and chlorophyll can be obtained to mix with corn or wheat to make bread, etc. and can be used as a food for poultry or livestock. It's a lot of work though, so you probably don't want to try it at home. A high-quality paper can be made from the fiber. Scientists have found that water hyacinth will purify polluted water, so sewage treatment plants are using it; methane gas can be produced from fermentation of the plant. For the moment it remains another under-utilized natural resource.

Cool fact: The water hyacinth extracts solids and metals from the water in which it lives. NASA has come up with a way to extract precious metals from the harvested plants. Thar's gold in them thar weeds!!

What other plants start with W?

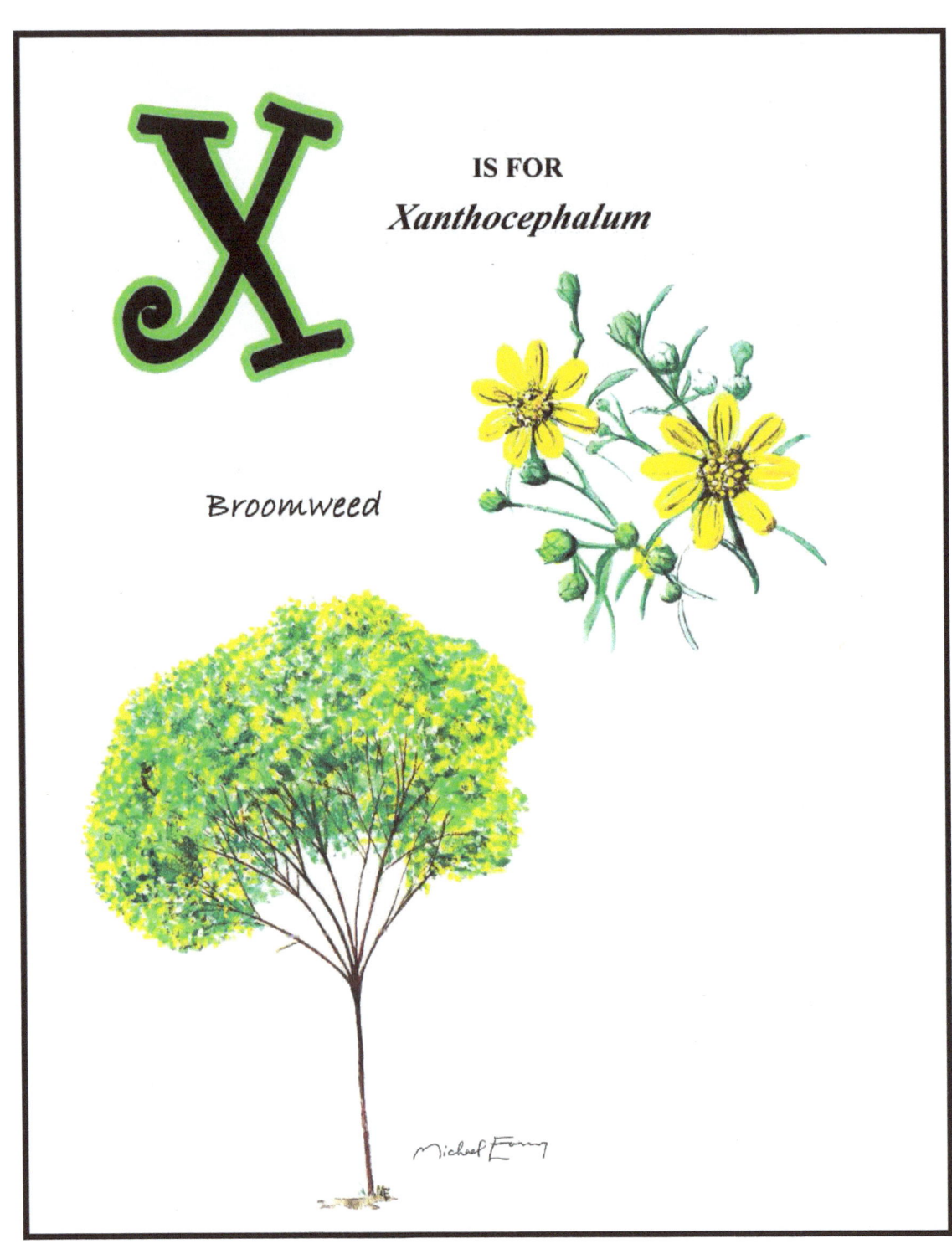

X IS FOR *Xanthocephalum*

Broomweed

Xanthocephalum (broomweed) in general is a group of plants best left alone unless you are into dye-making; allergic reactions and dermatitis are reasons enough and livestock poisoning from eating broomweed and cocklebur add to that, if you have lifestock. Both broomweed and cocklebur are in the huge Asteraceae (sunflower) family and while the cocklebur, which irritatingly hooks onto your clothes, does produce medicines for a wide variety of ailments, broomweed does not. There are a number of plants named broomweed that do, though they belong to different families.

Aside from the fact that it once was used to make brooms and does have a pretty yellow flower, there's not much to recommend it. Still, given that the sunflower family is so large and delivers so much, we should expect there to be a black sheep or two.

Cool fact: The broomweed, *Gutierrezia sarothrae*, is described as being used for a great many ills by Blackfoot, Lakota, Dakota, Zuni and other Native American tribes, but unless you decide, like the Navajo, to rub the ashes on your body to treat a headache or dizziness, you won't be adding it to the medicine cabinet.

What other plant begins with X?

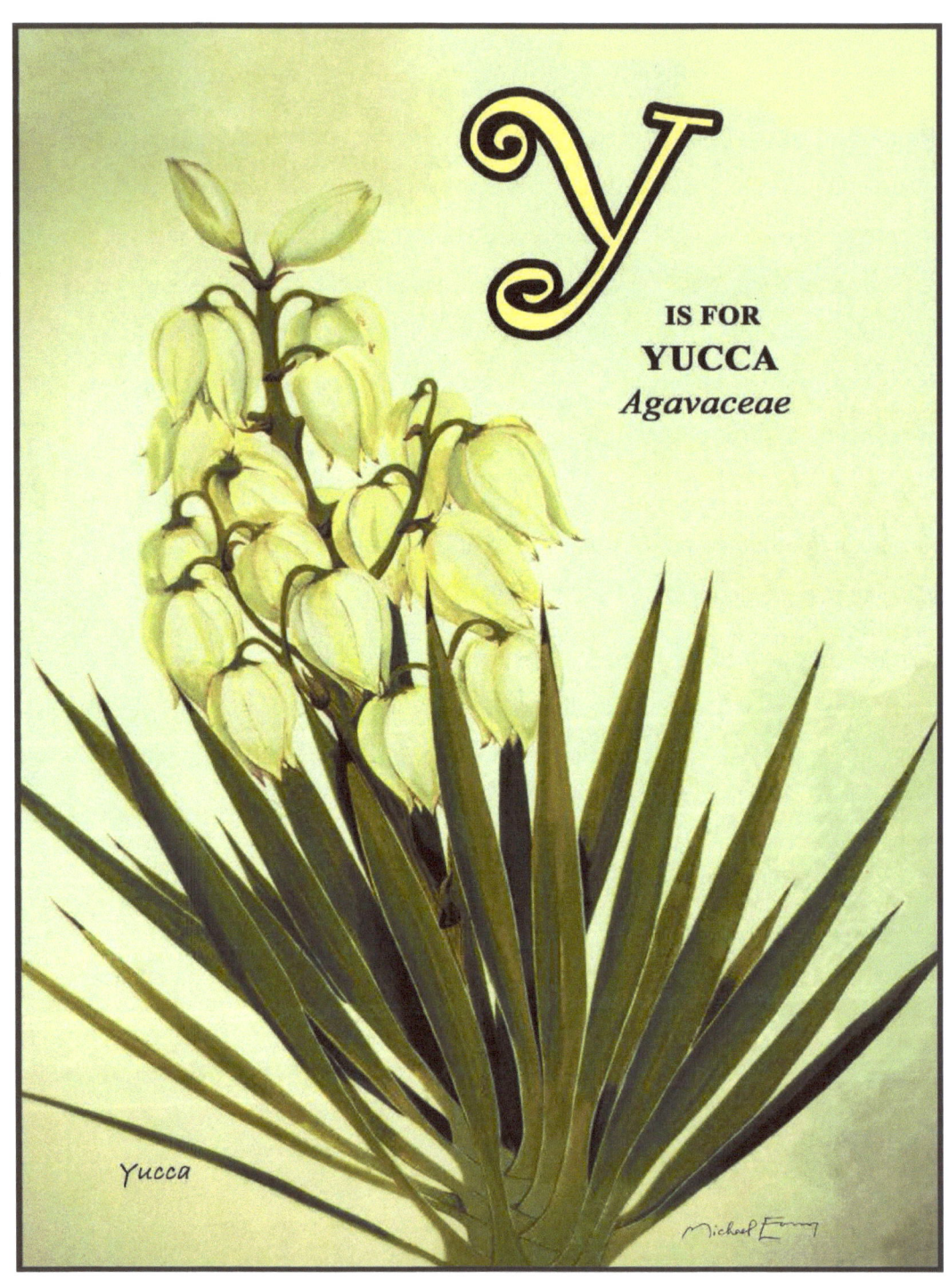

Yuccas still provide food to many in Mexico. You might see a lady walking down the road with a stalk, heavy with white flowers. She is either taking it to market or home to feed her family. The petals, which are high in vitamin C, may be separated from the green center which can be bitter in some species; they add a nice touch to salads, sauté or fry them with other vegetables. If you can get there before the deer munch on them, the young flowering stalk can be cooked, though the outer skin may need to be peeled. When the fruit is ripe it too can be eaten; again, you will have to sample the different species, as some have tough, woody fruits. Baskets, mats and thatching are still made with Yucca leaves, and the tall stems, after they are dry, make fencing and provide fuel for cooking and heating in more remote parts of Mexico. The Yucca root makes a shampoo or soap that was used for thousands of years by Native Americans. Since obtaining the root means killing the plant, better you stick to manufactured cleansers.

Cool fact: For millions of years the yucca moth, *Tegeticulla yuccasella*, and the yucca, *Yucca glauca*, have depended upon each other for survival. Taking the pollen from one flower, the moth goes to another where she lays her eggs. That flower is now pollinated, and when the eggs hatch the larva feed on the seeds resulting from the pollination, the larva leave enough uneaten seeds to grow into more Yuccas. One cannot live without the other.

What other plant starts with Y?

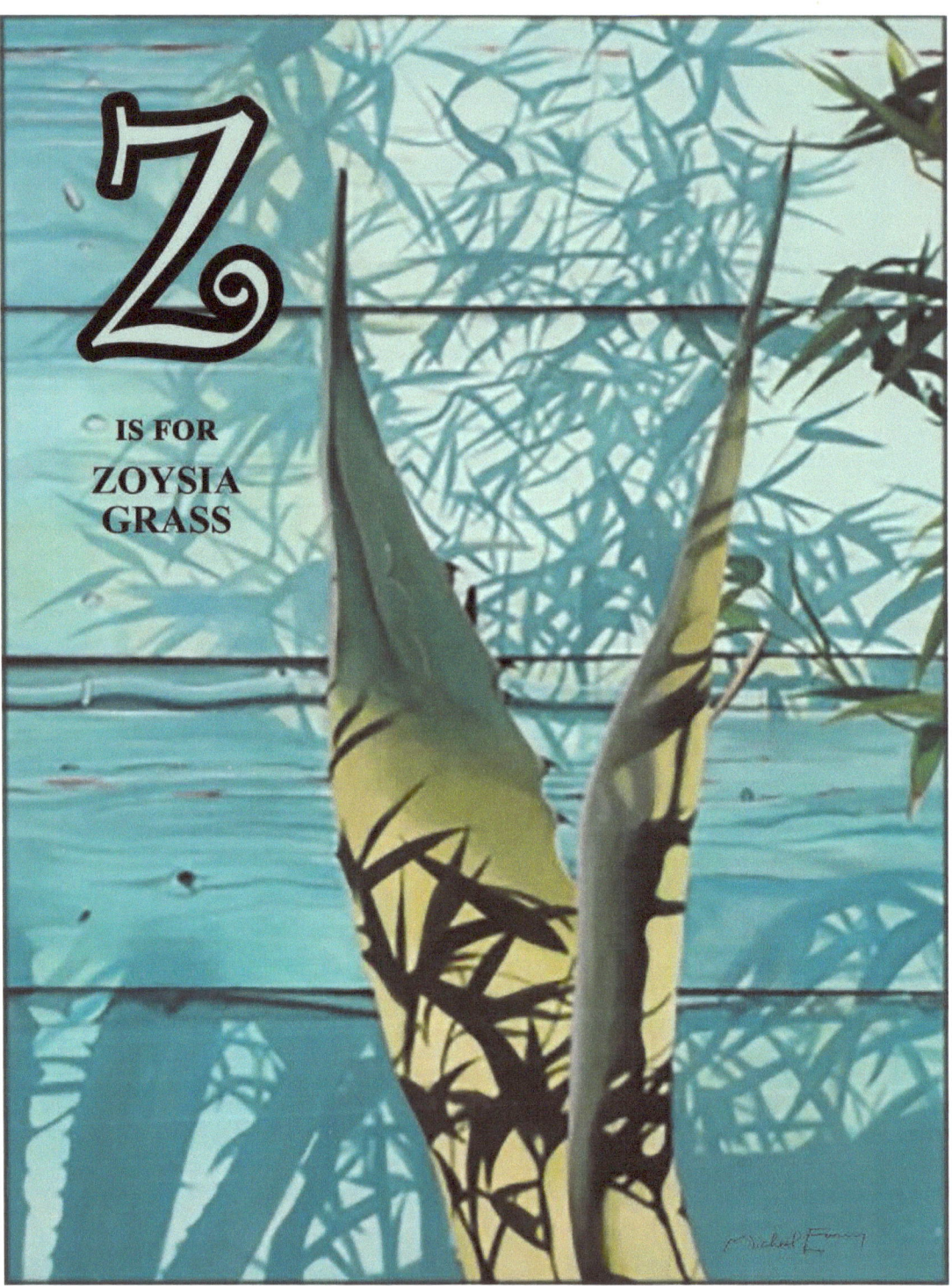

Zoysiagrass is our introduction to all the grasses. Native to southeast and east Asia, it has become very popular as a lawn grass because it forms a dense spreading turf. Its spreading ability has resulted in its taking hold in the wild. When we go outside, unless we are standing on paving, rock or sand, we are most likely standing on grass. Almost half of the United States is covered with grasses, a class of plants only outnumbered by the sunflower family and the orchid family. The grains we eat, wheat, barley, oats, rice, and corn, are all cultivated grasses. So why eat grass when all these cultivated versions are available? You just might like it. We don't have two stomachs like cows so it would be better to drink it. Wheatgrass is a popular drink, touted for its great health benefits. So you could cut some young grass – not the lawn, remember it has very likely been doused with herbicides – juice it along with wild grass seeds, which are smaller but essentially the same as their cultivated cousins, and give it a try. So what's with the picture of an agave? It's not a grass, you say. Look at the shadows. Bamboo leaves, and yes, you got it, bamboo is a grass.

Cool fact: Certain species of bamboo can grow 35 inches in 24 hours. There are 1450 species, one of which grows to 98 feet and nearly eight inches in diameter. There is one species of bamboo that will flower only once at intervals from 65 to 130 years; every plant of the same stock, no matter its geographical location, flowers at the same time, then dies.

What other plant starts with Z?

Wild Rose

Rosaceae

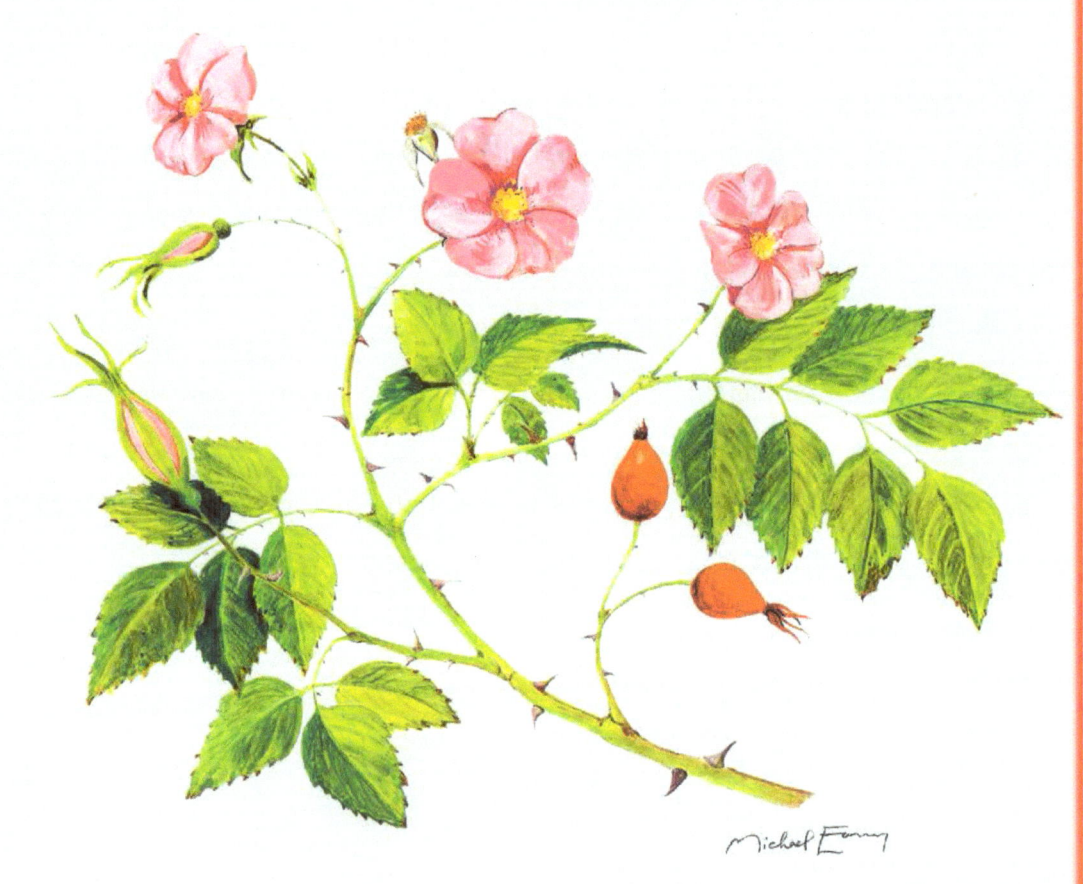

Author's Note

In order to present the alphabet using some of my older paintings as well as those painted especially for this book, I employed Latin, common and not-so-common names. Consequentially, if you are looking for Strawberry, for instance, you will find it under F for *Fragaria*, not S. To placate those that are easily upset by such things, here's an extra: the Wild Rose (*Rosaceae*)

Three rose hips (the fruit of the rose plant) contain as much vitamin C as one orange as well as vitamins A, E, and P. A delicious tea can be made from both the petals and the hips. The roots and leaves can also be used in teas. Fresh petals can be added to salads, made into jelly or candy. Gathered in the fall, rose hips can be dried for future use. Rose hip jelly, using three parts hips to one part sour apples, is another way to get the benefits of the rose. Rose hip syrup is given to children and invalids. It helps grow healthy bones, teeth and tissue.

Cool fact: It has been suggested, with good supporting evidence, that the sequence in "Alice in Wonderland", when Alice finds the royal gardeners painting the white roses red, is a reference to the War of the Roses (1455-1485). One of the gardeners explains that if the Red Queen were to see a white rose, she would have their heads cut off. Which recalls Shakespeare's "Henry VI" wherein Queen Margaret of the House of Lancaster, the White House, having the captive Duke of York, the Red House, in her power, says, "Off with his head!" just as Lewis Carroll's Red Queen does all the time.

Gertrude Stein famously said, "A rose is a rose is a rose."

Bibliography

Tull, Delena, 2013, *Edible and Useful Plants of the Southwest: Texas, New Mexico, and Arizona*, University of Texas Press

Nyerges, Christopher, 1997, *Guide to Wild Foods*, Survival News Service

Jones, Pamela, 1991, *Just Weeds*, Prentice Hall Press

Gibbons, Euell, 1971, *Stalking the Healthful Herbs and Stalking the Wild Asparagus*, David McKay Company

Vines, Robert, 1986, *Trees, Shrubs and Woody Vines of the Southwest*, University of Texas Press

Ritchason, Jack, 1995, *The Little Herb Encyclopedia*, Woodland Health

Angier, Bradford, 1974, *Books, Field Guide to Edible Wild Plants,* Stackpole Books

Harrington, H. D., 1972, *Western Edible Wild Plants*, University of New Mexico Press

Bianchini, Francesco, 1977, *Health Plants of the World*, Newsweek Books

Niethammer, Mildred, 1974 *Plant Medicine and Folklore*, Macmillan

Swerdlow, Joel L., *Nature's Medicines*, National Geographic

Lehane, Brendan, *The Power of Plants*, McGraw-Hill

Young, Dan, Vanderbilt Press, Stephenville, Texas

And the many more read and learned from over the years but not directly referenced for this book.

More A to Z Weeds

A: agave, amaranth, apple

B: bee balm, barberry, blueberry
C: crocus, clover, cactus
D: daisy, dewberry, dock

E: evening primrose, elm, elephant ear
F: foxglove, fennel, farkleberry
G: golden rod, goosefoot, greenthread
H: horehound, hemp, henbit
I: inky cap, indian ricegrass, iris
J: jasmine, jimsonweed, jujube
K: knotweed, kinnikinik, killwort
L: lambs tongue, lantana, lily
M: milkweed, mallow, maple

N: nightshade, nasturtium, navajo tea
O: ocotillo, oxalis, onion
P: palm, passionflower, pecan
Q: quick grass
R: ragweed, radish, ramps
S: sage, saltbush, sumac
T: tomatillo, tumbleweed
U: uva ursi, umbrella-tree
V: verbena, vetch, violet
W: walnut, willow, wormwood
X: xic-che, xocat, xkanlol
Y: yaupon, yew

Z: zorilla, zexmenia

If you enjoyed this book, Michael P. Earney would be most appreciative if you would leave a review on Amazon, Goodreads, or any other Review site you like.

Also, don't forget to tell your friends! Word of mouth advertising is the most precious Thank You, a reader could give to an author.

Visit www.MichaelEarney.com to learn more about this author's books and various achievements.

www.ingramcontent.com/pod-product-compliance
Lightning Source LLC
Chambersburg PA
CBHW051206220526
45473CB00003B/921